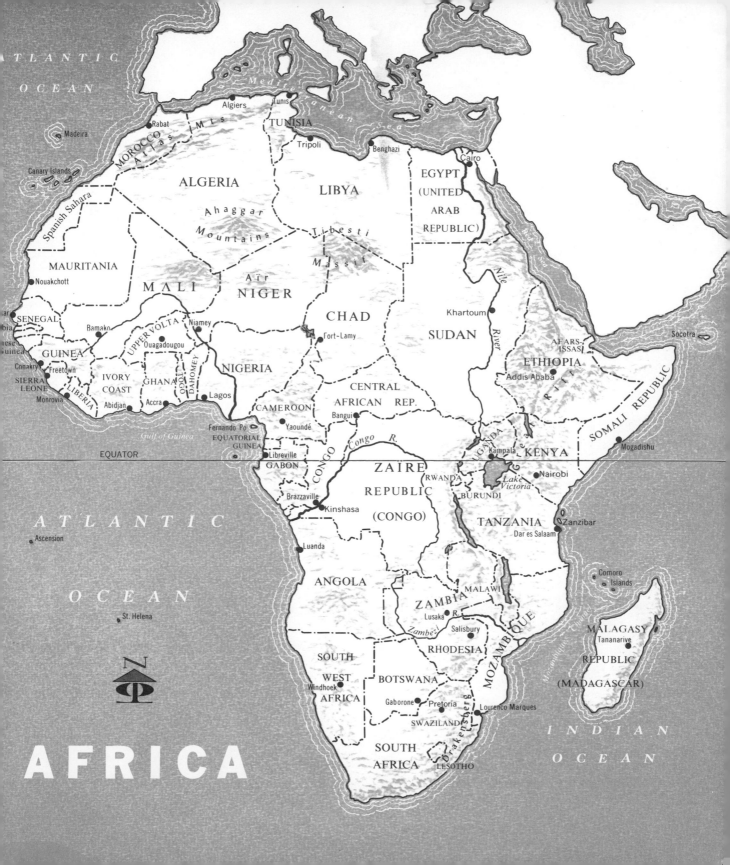

Enchantment of Africa

KENYA

E. S. E. A.
TITLE II

by ALLAN CARPENTER
and MILAN DE LANY

Consulting Editor
David Rubadiri, M.A.
African Studies Faculty
Northwestern University
Evanston, Illinois

 CHILDRENS PRESS, CHICAGO

THE ENCHANTMENT OF AFRICA

Available now: Botswana, Egypt (United Arab Republic), Kenya, Malagasy Republic (Madagascar), Zambia.
Planned for the future, six each season: Algeria, Burundi, Cameroon, Central African Republic, Chad, Congo (Brazzaville), Dahomey, Equatorial Guinea, Ethiopia, Gabon, Gambia, Ghana, Guinea, Ivory Coast, Lesotho, Liberia, Libya, Malawi, Mali, Mauritania, Morocco, Niger, Nigeria, Rhodesia, Rwanda, Senegal, Sierra Leone, Somali Republic, South Africa, South West Africa, Sudan, Tanzania, Togo, Tunisia, Uganda, Upper Volta, Zaïre Republic (Congo Kinshasha)

ACKNOWLEDGMENTS

Robinson McIlvaine, Ambassador of the United States of America, Nairobi, Kenya; Frank K. Njagi, Ministry of Information and Broadcasting, Nairobi, Kenya; Embassy of the Republic of Kenya, Washington, D.C.; Robert G. Cushing, Director, U.S. Information Service, Nairobi, Kenya

Cover Photograph: Zebras at Nairobi National Park, Allan Carpenter
Frontispiece: Arab dhows in the old harbor at Mombasa, Wildlife and Safari in Kenya

Series Coordinator: Michael Roberts
Project Editor: Joan Downing
Assistant Editor: Janis Fortman
Manuscript Editor: Elizabeth Rhein
Map Artist: Donald G. Bouma

LIBRARY OF CONGRESS
CATALOGING IN PUBLICATION DATA

Carpenter, John Allan, 1917-
  Kenya.
  (Enchantment of Africa)

  SUMMARY: An introduction to the geography, history, people, culture, industries, and attractions of Kenya.
  1. Kenya—Juvenile literature. [1. Kenya.]
I. De Lany, Milan, joint author. II. Title.
DT 433.5.C37   915.76'2   72–10708
ISBN 0–516–04566–0

Contents

A True Story to Set the Scene

THE MAN-EATERS OF TSAVO

Kenya badly needed a railroad that would connect it with Uganda; in 1895 this railroad was begun. Its completion would mean a great deal to Kenya. Before work could progress, though, a strange occurrence had to be stopped.

At a point about 135 miles from the city of Mombasa, the Tsavo River had to be crossed in order for the railroad to continue inland. Building the bridge would be a difficult undertaking since the area was jungle and there were few supplies and only limited help. The biggest obstacle, however, was a tragic adventure that delayed the project for nine full months.

Colonel J. H. Patterson, the chief engineer in charge of the construction of the railway, went to the town of Tsavo to supervise construction of the bridge. He spent the first night sleeping peacefully in a small grass shack. Had he known that two savage, man-eating lions were prowling around seeking their victim, his sleep would not have been so peaceful. The two lions would be in the area for over nine months before they were killed. They terrorized the workers and completely halted railroad construction. The lions became so good at taking victims that the workers began to believe that they were demons rather than amimals.

One night a man named Unga Singh, one of the Indian overseers, was dragged out of his tent by one of the lions. Because efforts by Colonel Patterson to trail the lion failed, the colonel sat up all the next

The man-eating lions of Tsavo terrorized workers and halted construction of the railroad.

night in a tree near Unga Singh's tent. He wanted to see if the animal would come back again. With his rifle and shotgun ready, Colonel Patterson waited and waited. Near midnight he heard the ominous roar of the brutes—and then silence. Shortly afterward he heard commotion farther away in another camp. Before anyone could prevent it, the lions had taken another victim. The next night Patterson spent in a tree near that tent, tying a goat to the base of the tree to attract the lions. Again the beasts eluded him and struck in still another camp.

Another time one of the lions ventured into a railroad car parked on the siding, taking its victim from among workers who were sleeping there. After a while nothing frightened these lions, and they showed complete contempt for man. Having once chosen their victim, the lions allowed nothing to keep them from capturing him. They soon were not satisfied with only one victim a night. The situation grew so bad that one day most of the Indian laborers stopped the first train going to the coast, piled in, and fled. The very few who remained at Tsavo were busy erecting "lion-proof " huts for themselves.

After many unsuccessful attempts to capture the lions, one of them was finally shot. News of the death of the notorious man-eater spread far and wide, and soon congratulations came pouring in. The other one, however, was still alive.

At last the second man-eater was shot by the patient and persistent Colonel Patterson, but only after many harrowing experiences and narrow escapes. The second lion measured nine feet, six inches from the tip of its nose to the tip of its tail.

The two man-eating lions that caused so much fear and so many deaths had the distinction of being mentioned in the British House of Lords by England's prime minister of that time, Lord Salisbury. During their reign of terror, the two lions had killed at least twenty-eight Indian workers and scores of unfortunate African natives. These two man-eating lions are preserved and on display at the Field Museum of Natural History in Chicago.

The Face of the Land

A beautiful, snow-covered mountain right on the equator, cool and fertile highlands, and clear, trout-filled mountain streams—all these are unexpected features of the enchanting tropical land of Kenya.

Located in east-central Africa, Kenya covers an area of 224,960 square miles, making it larger than the states of California and Florida combined. The Indian Ocean washes its eastern shores. The

Somali Republic borders Kenya on the northeast. Bordering Kenya on the north are Ethiopia and a very small portion of the Sudan. On the west Kenya is bound by the Republic of Uganda and the immense Lake Victoria. On the south the United Republic of Tanzania shares the longest stretch of Kenya's border.

CONTRASTS ON THE EQUATOR

Kenya is a land of contrasts. There are cool, fertile highlands in the southwest, where most of the people live, and sparsely inhabited semi-desert regions in the northeast. There are wild bushland and plains, called the *pori*, where countless wild animals roam. The coastal belt is hot and humid, but its evergreen coconut palms, mango trees, and cashew nut trees provide a pleasant relief. Here are delightful seaside resorts with clean, sandy beaches and good swimming. Deep-sea fishing is popular at offshore coral reefs.

THE GREAT RIFT VALLEY

An impressive geographical feature of Kenya, and of the whole of east Africa for that matter, is the stupendous Rift Valley (often called the Great Rift Valley). A *rift* is a depression or valley formed between two *faults* (fractures in the earth's crust that displace the earth around them, causing one side of the fracture to be lower than the other).

The Rift Valley is perhaps the longest rift in the world. This gigantic valley is said to begin in the Dead Sea in Israel, run southward through the Red Sea, then cut into and through Ethiopia. As it enters Kenya it splits into two great arms; one arm enters Kenya through Lake Rudolf in the northwest and the other circles the east African countries farther west. A chain of lakes is cradled in this huge valley, including some of the world's longest, such as Lake Tanganyika, 450 miles long. The eastern and western arms of the Rift Valley join again south of Tanzania. The

MAP KEY

Aberdare Range, D3	Kakamega, D1	Lake Naivasha, E2	Masai Amboseli Game Reserve, F3	Nakuru, D2
Athi River, E3	Kapsabet, D2	Lake Nakuru, D2	Masai Mara Game Reserve, E2	Namanga, F3
Buna, B5	Kericho, D2	Lake Rudolf, B2		Nanyuki, D3
Bura, E5	Kerio River, C2	Lake Victoria, E1	Mathews Range, C3	Nyeri, D3
Chalbi Desert, B3	Kibwezi, F4	Lamu, F6	Mombasa, G5	Olorgasailie, E2
Dawa River, A6	Kilifi, F5	Limuru, E3	Moyale, B4	Rift Valley, C2
Eldoret, D2	Kipini, F5	Lodwar, B2	Mt. Elgon, C1	Talta Hills, F4
El Wak, B5	Kisii, E1	Lokichokio, A1	Mt. Kenya, D3	Tana River, D4
Embu, D3	Kisumu, D1	Lokitaung, A2	Mt. Kenya National Park, D3	Thika, E3
Ewaso Ng'iro, E2	Kitale, C2	Lorian Swamp, D5		Timboroa, D2
Formosa Bay, F5	Kolbio, E6	Mado Gashi, D4	Mt. Kulal, B3	Thomsons Falls, D2
Fort Hall, E3	Kwale, G5	Magadi, E3	Mt. Longonot, E3	Tsavo, F4
Fort Ternan, D2	Laisamis, C3	Malindi, F5	Mt. Nyiru, C3	Tsavo National Park, F4
Galana River, F4	Lake Baringo, D2	Mandera, B6	Mt. Suswa, E2	
Galole, E5	Lake Elmenteita, D2	Mara River, E2	Nairobi, E3	Tsavo River, F4
Garissa, D5		Maralal, C2	Nairobi National Park, E3	Turkwel River, C2
Garsen, F5	Lake Hannington, D2	Marsabit, C3		Uasa Nyira, D4
Huri Hills, B3		Marsabit National Reserve, B4	Naivasha, E3	Voi, F4
Isiolo, D3	Lake Magadi, E3			Wajir, C5

*Desertlike regions
in the northeast;
cool, fertile highlands
in the southwest;
the great Rift Valley;
wild bushland or* pori*;
the hot, lush coastal
belt—Kenya is a
land of contrasts.
Right: Thomsons Falls
in the Rift Valley.
Below: Natives
in the highlands.*

3,500-mile-long Rift Valley then comes to an end as it runs through the Zambezi River gorge into the Indian Ocean.

This rift forms the main geological feature of Kenya, and in a way of the whole African continent. There are cliffs with steep sides that drop two to three thousand feet into the valley below. At the bottom the rift averages forty miles wide; in some areas farms and ranches flourish on the valley floor. Though geologists do not seem to agree as to the origin of the Rift Valley, it probably came into being during some tremendous upheaval of the earth's crust in prehistoric times.

On the floor of the Rift Valley about fifty miles north of Nairobi is a hill called Mount Margaret; it is near the extinct volcanoes of Mount Suswa and Mount Longonot. In 1971 space scientists set up a satellite tracking station on top of this hill. Sponsored by the East African External Telecommunications, Ltd., this station sends messages across one-third of the earth's surface by way of an Intelstat communication satellite, located about 22,500 miles above the Indian Ocean.

THE HIGHLANDS

The very attractive and fertile highlands, from the central regions to the southwest, cover only about one-fourth of Kenya. The altitude of this region ranges from four to ten thousand feet above sea level. The climate here is very pleasant. Because of the altitude, temperatures range from forty to eighty degrees Fahrenheit, even though this is a tropical region very near the equator. Rainfall in the highlands varies from thirty to eighty inches or more a year. For these reasons the highland region is a very desirable area for settlement. Africans and Europeans alike established farms and developed the highlands, making this region the backbone of Kenya's economy. With the exception of three or four coastal towns, it is in the highlands that the larger towns and cities are located. Nairobi, the capital of Kenya, is one of these cities. Located at the gateway to the highlands, it is 5,500 feet above sea level. The nights are cool, humidity is low, and the temperature rarely exceeds eighty degrees. It is a most attractive modern city with a population of over five hundred thousand.

THE COAST AND THE LOWLANDS

The low-lying coastal strip is fairly heavily populated. Besides coastal resort towns, there are sizable coconut and cashew nut plantations. Even pineapples have been grown successfully here.

A little farther inland is a wider strip, eighty to one hundred miles wide in some places, consisting of thick, not easily penetrable thorny bushland with very little water. Wild animals such as lions, rhinoceroses, elephants, giraffes, antelopes, and many others have found their protection in this region called the *pori*. In the early days of Kenya's history, this forbidding

Along with other wild animals, antelope roam the grassy, treeless, open plains.

barrier of thornbush discouraged early visitors from penetrating into the interior or "hinterland."

Because of the lower altitudes the climate in the pori is warm. The rainfall, however, is scant—only about ten to twenty inches per year. This is the natural abode of Kenya's great wealth of big game and many other animals. Because of this, many of the game parks are located in this region.

About halfway between the seaport of Mombasa and the highland city of Nairobi rises a large cluster of high hills, called the Talta Hills. Looking very much like Switzerland, this region of streams and green valleys provides a most pleasant setting for the homes of the Talta people. Vegetables, bananas, and poultry from the Talta Hills go to the markets of Mombasa.

The road approaching Nairobi winds for about forty miles through great stretches of grassy, open plains. Hardly a tree can be seen, and herds of gnu, kongoni, zebra, antelope, and some ostrich roam in the open.

THE SEMIDESERT

The northern and northeastern region of Kenya is barren and dry. A water hole is rare and very valuable. North of the Tana River this semidesert region is very sparsely inhabited. Here and there nomadic tribesmen take their cattle and goats, and occasionally camels, through miles of scrubland to find grazing land. Strangely enough, ownership of this inhospitable area was once contested heavily by the Somalis across the border, and occasionally there have been border skirmishes between Somali and Kenyan patrols. Somalia would have liked to annex this portion of Kenya.

Though the semidesert regions in the north are quite flat, there are isolated ranges and peaks that unexpectedly rise out of the low-lying country. Because of very minimal rainfall, they look somewhat stark in their lonesome setting. Among the notable peaks are the Mathews Range, Marsabit Mountain, which has been declared a national park, and Mount Kulal at the southern shore of Lake Rudolf.

MOUNTAINS AND RANGES

Kenya got its name from the impressive, snow-covered Mount Kenya, which towers 17,058 feet into the blue skies. It is the second highest mountain on the continent of Africa. It is also higher than the highest mountains in the United States, except for Mount McKinley in Alaska which is 20,320 feet high.

The equator passes through the northern slopes of Mount Kenya. Only in South America can be seen such an unusual feature as is present on this mountain on the equator—a covering of snow all year. There are no fewer than twelve glaciers on Mount Kenya's twin peaks of Batian and Nellion.

Mount Kenya was first discovered for the outside world in 1849 by Dr. J. L. Krapf, the missionary-explorer. A year earlier his colleague, Johann Rebmann, had seen the massive peak of Mount Kilimanjaro in northern Tanzania. When these two missionaries first reported in their letters to Europe that they had seen snow-covered mountains in those regions, their reports were ridiculed as mere figments of the imagination. Later, other European explorers were sent out to verify these claims.

The lower slopes of Mount Kenya are covered with thick forest. Below this forest belt live the Kikuyu people, the largest ethnic group in Kenya. Stretching westward across the Aberdare Range are the famous Kenya highlands. Mount Kenya, in the center of the country, stands as a gigantic sentinel on the dividing line of the highlands and the lowlands.

The second highest mountain is Mount Elgon, 14,178 feet high. At certain times of the year snow can be seen on this mountain as well, but it does not stay there long. Like Mount Kenya, it is an extinct volcano, and it is located on the northwest border between Kenya and Uganda.

The Aberdare Range extends northward from Nairobi for about one hundred miles. The highest point in this range is 13,104 feet. Its slopes are thickly covered with forest, including bamboo forests that are almost impenetrable. Above the forest line are very attractive plains. A road has been built over the top of the Aberdares, and it is one of the most scenic routes in Africa. The western slopes of the Aberdares descend steeply into the Rift Valley.

LAKES

Most of the lakes of Kenya are in the eastern branch of the Rift Valley. The largest of these is Lake Rudolf. It stretches for 180 miles north to the Ethiopian border, and at its widest point measures thirty-seven miles. The water of Lake Rudolf is brackish but drinkable. As this lake is surrounded by arid plains, there are very few trees in the area and the climate is hot. In recent years a fishery has been started, but what is most exciting are recent findings of remnants of prehistoric man, which will draw scientists and anthropologists into that area.

South of Lake Rudolf is a chain of smaller lakes nestled in the Rift Valley. They are Lake Baringo, Lake Hannington, Lake Nakuru, Lake Elmenteita, and Lake Naivasha. The first four lakes are the habitat of millions of colorful pink flamingos. These long-legged birds look like pink clouds when in flight. Lake Nakuru has so many birds that it has been proclaimed a bird sanctuary.

Near the southern border with Tanzania is Lake Magadi. The water in this lake is very brackish and salty, and the shoreline has large deposits of soda and salt. These deposits have been so profitable that the railroad was extended to the lake to haul away the mined salt and soda.

Not to be forgotten is the eastern portion of Lake Victoria, the largest lake in Africa. It is actually an inland sea, covering 24,300 square miles, and is shared by the countries of Kenya, Uganda, and Tanzania. There is a steamer service on Lake Victoria, and Kenya's main port on the lake is Kisumu.

When the millions of flamingos on Lake Nakuru are in flight, they look like pink clouds.

The Tana River is the major obstacle on the cattle drive from Somalia to Mombasa. Cattle cross the river in small groups in case some are swept away by the strong current. Some Somalis and local tribesmen swim alongside the cattle to coax them across, while others in dugout canoes prod the cattle on the bank.

RIVERS

In the highlands many small streams form watersheds. Most of them rise in the Aberdares and the slopes of Mount Kenya and ultimately flow east into the Indian Ocean. Many of these streams drain into the Tana River, Kenya's largest. Eventually the Tana flows into the Indian Ocean near Kipini.

Unfortunately the Tana is not navigable; only for a short distance near the coast is it navigable by canoe or launch. Before it slows down in the lowlands, the Tana travels swiftly through deep valleys and gorges. Plans have been made to harness this river by building dams where hydroelectric plants can be installed to supply electricity. Such dams would make irrigation possible as well.

A smaller river, the Athi, winds through the plains and eventually joins the Tsavo River, which flows from the slopes of Mount Kilimanjaro into Kenya. This becomes the Galana River and flows into the Indian Ocean just north of Malindi. It is navigable for a short distance only by canoe.

The Tana and the Athi-Galana are the two main rivers of Kenya. A third river flowing east is the Uasa Nyira, which originates on the northern slopes of Mount Kenya. It has a seemingly promising start, but disappears into the vast Lorian Swamp in the semi-arid northeast regions. A few smaller rivers flow from the western ranges along the Rift Valley and into Lake Victoria. Two rivers, the Kerio and the Turkwel, flow north into Lake Rudolf.

In most of the lakes and the larger rivers of Kenya, crocodiles and hippopotamuses make themselves at home. This can be dangerous for the unwary stranger who takes a swim in unfamiliar waters.

Five Children of Kenya

NJOROGE FROM NYERI

A modest stone house with a corrugated iron roof, surrounded by a banana grove and a small garden, is the home of a Kikuyu boy named Njoroge. His home is located in Nyeri, the scenic community on the slopes of Mount Kenya where many Kikuyu people live. Njoroge is the oldest in a family of five children. He had to learn early in life to help in the garden and take the goats to pasture.

The food Njoroge eats is quite different from what American children eat. One popular dish called *irio* consists of mashed red kidney beans and whole hominy,

Njoroge lives in a modest stone house like this one in a Kikuyu village near Mount Kenya.

boiled together until thick. Wrapped in banana leaves, irio is a popular food to take along on a trip. Another well-liked dish is cornmeal mush. It is somewhat like grits, and is sometimes served with meat

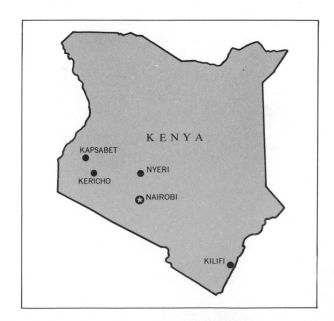

19

Njoroge's father teaches in a primary school like this one. Boys wear shirts and khaki shorts to school, while girls wear dresses. All of the students go barefoot.

stew. Green unripe bananas, cut into cubes and boiled, serve as the main starchy food.

Njoroge's father, a teacher in a nearby primary school, is anxious for his children to get good educations. When Njoroge was seven years old, he started going to the school where his father taught. He was a bright boy and eager to learn about many things, including other people and other parts of the world. Both during and after school, the boys wear shirts and khaki shorts, while the girls wear simple dresses. It is a custom for the children to go barefoot.

One day Njoroge learned about the activities of a local Boy Scout troop. It was

not long before he joined the troop. He immediately began to participate in all their activities. Sometimes they went up into the dense forest on hikes and saw all sorts of wild animals. Njoroge soon earned several merit badges of which he was very proud.

One day there was a lot of excitement at the troop meeting. A Scout leader from Nairobi came to visit Njoroge's troop on a special mission. He was to choose a few of the best Scouts to attend the annual World Scouting Jamboree to be held in a foreign country. Imagine how Njoroge felt when he was told that he was one of the Scouts who had been chosen to go! When it finally came time to leave for the jamboree,

Njoroge was so excited that he could hardly pack his uniform and other needs in his little bag.

Njoroge met Scouts from many lands at the jamboree. One evening a group of them sat around a campfire telling of their experiences. As one of the few Scouts from Kenya, Njoroge was asked many questions about his native land. He told his new friends about the founder of the World Boy Scouts, Lord Baden-Powell. This great man had been all over the world and chose to retire in the beautiful community of Nyeri. He lived there until he died in 1941. His grave, in a little cemetery in Nyeri, has a simple but descriptive tombstone. Njoroge's new friends were impressed when he told them that for years it had been a privileged duty of the Nyeri Boy Scouts to tend Lord Baden-Powell's grave and to keep it clean and tidy.

When Njoroge returned from the jamboree he began wondering what he should do as an adult. His horizons had been widened and he had seen new places and met many people of different races. He thinks he probably would like to become a teacher like his father, only he wants to get a college education first and then teach in a secondary school or college.

MARGIE FROM KERICHO

Margie is an English girl who is growing up among the Kipsigis people in Kericho, the growing tea capital of Kenya. Her parents are English tea planters who became citizens of Kenya after independence.

Margie is able to make friends easily. Even though her parents are quite well-to-do and have a comfortable English-type home with a cozy fireplace, she likes to visit her African friends, some of whom live in simple huts. She learned to speak both Swahili and Kipsigis at a very early age, along with English, which is spoken by her parents.

Margie's playmates have taught her many different games and activities. One

Margie likes to watch Kipsigis girls weaving colorful blankets.

KENYA INFORMATION SERVICES

game that she especially likes is called *cholo*. Opponents move bean pods in two rows of hollows carved in a board. The winner is the one who can wipe out all of his opponent's beans. Margie also watches the Kipsigis girls weave pretty, colorful baskets and mats or fashion cooking pots out of clay. Margie has even made a few of these pots herself.

At times Margie's African friends bring her some baby wild animals that they catch. She is delighted to get them, and she raises them as pets. Among these are two small antelopes that she first nursed with a milk bottle. They became cute and playful as they grew older. They follow her around everywhere and get peanuts from her.

Her favorite is the little night monkey, or "bush baby," she has named "Lemi." Lemi has big ears, big eyes, velvety fur, and a longish, curled tail. His tiny hands are almost like human hands. Lemi likes to suck at a bit of cloth that has been dipped in milk and sometimes nibbles at a banana. Most of all he likes little insects such as grasshoppers. Margie is kept busy looking for grasshoppers to feed him. Lemi sometimes curls up in a little woven basket Margie has placed on her windowsill.

Perhaps her strangest pet is a chameleon with three horns. Some of her African friends think it will bite them and are a bit afraid of it. The chameleon is harmless, however, and it crawls on Margie's arm and fingers, hoping to find a fly to eat.

Margie does not spend all her time playing with her friends and pets. She goes to a boarding school in Nairobi. Her school is in session for three months, followed by a one-month vacation. Then she goes back to school again for three months, and home for another month of vacation.

Margie is interested in the varied customs of the peoples of Kenya. As she speaks Swahili well, she has decided that someday she will visit all of Kenya, study the customs, take a lot of pictures, and then write a book about the country. She does not want people to forget about the old ways.

KIPTUM FROM KAPSABET

A young boy is pensively watching a herd of cattle belonging to his father. It is cold outside, for this is the plateau region of Kapsabet—about seven thousand feet above sea level. Kiptum doesn't mind the cold, though, for he likes the outdoor life —the bracing air, the bright sunshine, birds and butterflies flitting about here and there. Sometimes he sees a wild hare and has great fun trying to outrun it.

Being a Nandi boy Kiptum follows many of the old traditions of his elders. Recently he acquired a spear; with other boys his own age, he became very adept at throwing the spear at targets quite a distance away. Following a gentler pursuit, he plays his little music box, the *mbira*. Each of its flat strips is tuned to a different

*Kiptum enjoys watching
his elders perform
traditional dances.*

pitch. He twangs the strips with his thumbs, producing lively tunes. Sometimes one of the shy, young village girls passing by with a water jar stops to listen.

At the beginning of the rainy season, the termites come out of their underground nests and fly in their ecstatic flight that leads to their mating. The termites pair off, with the male following the female. Then they drop their wings and find a place to start a new colony. While they are out flying, Kiptum and his friends delight in gathering around such a hole and snatching these big, juicy termites.

With nimble fingers the children fill their mouths and have a great feast. Kiptum and his friends are not the only ones who enjoy a meal of flying termites, for these insects are considered a delicacy among many Africans in Kenya.

Kiptum enjoys watching his elders perform traditional dances. Some of these are ceremonial dances, while others are old war dances accompanied by songs praising the prowess of warriors long ago. For those occasions the dancers put on fancy headdresses with ostrich plumes, adorn themselves with beads and bangles, and wear a broad belt of shells. On their ankles are little bells that tinkle rhythmically to their dance steps. These dancers are good athletes as well; they are especially good at running and jumping.

Before Kiptum could be accepted as an equal among the ranks of these young men and join them in their ceremonial dances, he had to go through a ceremony to be initiated into manhood. This rite took place when he was fourteen years old. It was primarily a test of his courage. During the circumcision rite, his face was watched intently to see if he flinched or uttered a cry of pain. After that he spent several days in the woods with other boys of his age. They had to fend for themselves, sleep in the open, find food as best they could, and protect themselves from dangerous animals. At certain appointed times the boys met with elders who instructed and initiated them in various facts of life.

Kiptum has always dreamed of being a great athlete someday. He has heard of young men from his tribe who were so good in certain athletic events, especially running, that the government chose some of them to represent Kenya at great world athletic competitions such as the Olympic Games. There some of them established new world records and came back home with silver and gold medals.

Kiptum has not had much schooling. He has learned to read and write a little, but most of his time is spent in the outdoors. As he grows up, he will probably follow in his father's footsteps and join the Kenya Armed Forces. If he does well in training

as a soldier and draws attention to his ability in running and jumping, his superiors might mark him for special training. Who knows? Someday he, too, might represent Kenya at the Olympics. His practice chasing hares as a boy might come in handy!

Kiptum knows he will marry when he gets older. He thinks he would like to marry a certain pretty girl who listens to him playing the mbira. When the time comes to ask her to be his wife, Kiptum will have to ask her father's permission. That would involve arrangements for a brideprice that Kiptum would have to pay, since his people believe that when a daughter marries, her family must be compensated for losing her. What would the brideprice amount to? Most likely it would include several cows, perhaps some goats, and also a certain sum of money. Kiptum is sure that it would be worth it, however, and he will do his best to earn it all, though perhaps his father might help him a little.

In doing this, Kiptum would be following the customs of his forefathers. To him that would be a happy life.

MOOLJI FROM NAIROBI

Even though Moolji lives in Nairobi, the capital of Kenya, all his playmates are Indian boys and girls. He attends an all-Indian school, follows the Moslem faith, and on Fridays attends religious services with his parents at the large mosque.

The store that Moolji's father owns is located on one of the main streets of Nairobi.

ALLAN CARPENTER

Moolji's father owns a general store on one of the main streets of Nairobi. It is a large store and the salesmen there are very courteous. People find it a pleasure to shop there, so business is good. When Moolji is home from school he helps his father in the store by running errands, arranging boxes, unpacking cartons, and doing whatever needs to be done. He is learning from experience what is involved in running a store.

When independence came to Kenya and the Africans took over the government, African students began to enroll at Moolji's school; it was no longer a purely Indian school. At first it was a bit hard for

Moolji to get used to, but before long he hardly noticed the changes. He learned about the customs of Africans and learned to speak the Swahili language. On one vacation he was invited by Maina, an African friend, to go to his home out in the country. This was quite a change from city life for Moolji, and he enjoyed it immensely. He learned a lot about country life and was fascinated by the chickens and goats in the yard of Maina's home.

While Moolji's horizons were expanding so quickly at school, his father and mother had to make a big decision. They had to choose whether they wanted citizenship in the new nation of Kenya or not. Since they

Moolji lives in a house like this one in Nairobi, surrounded by shrubs and flowers.

had lived in Kenya for many years and loved the nation and its people, they decided they would become citizens. They wanted to participate in what was being called "harambee"—pulling together to build the nation.

Moolji's house in Nairobi is surrounded by many shrubs and flowers. Moolji's mother likes to cook hot, spicy meals. Two of the family's favorite dishes are curried stew with rice and curried vegetables. Though curry can be very hot when a lot of curry powder is used, that is how Moolji's family likes their food. The curry powder that Moolji's mother uses is sent from India, along with mango chutney, a spicy seasoning made of mangoes, raisins, dates, and onions. Also served with family meals are sliced bananas and papayas, avocados, oranges, chopped peanuts, and fresh grated coconut.

Moolji is not the only child in his family; he has two brothers and two sisters. Moolji's sisters were married when they were quite young. His brothers, however, did not want to marry until they were established in their own professions or businesses. One of Moolji's brothers decided he would attend the University of Nairobi and become a lawyer. In a growing city like Nairobi a good lawyer is always needed. Because his other brother likes photography, he has thought about opening a studio in Nairobi someday. In addition to photographing people, he wants to make postcards of wild animal scenes. He knows that tourists would buy them.

What about Moolji? Since he has worked in his father's store all this time and likes that life, he plans to learn more about business by taking a business course at the University of Nairobi. He hopes that someday he can go into partnership with his father.

ASHA FROM A VILLAGE NEAR KILIFI

Half an hour's walk inland from the small coastal town of Kilifi, in a village where most of the huts are thatched with coconut palm leaves, lives a little Digo girl called Asha. She is a pretty girl and has learned to hold her body very straight, for Digo girls and women carry things by balancing them on their heads. It is always quite hot in the coastal area of Kenya, so all Asha wears is a simple grass skirt. Around her neck is a necklace made of tiny shells which she found on the beaches near Kilifi.

The village where Asha lives is built on a ridge. Thickets of thornbush stretch inland from the ridge for many miles. Looking eastward from her hut, Asha can see all the way to the Indian Ocean, with its white-capped waves glimmering in the sun. Silhouettes of coconut palms and huge mango trees make the view even more beautiful. In the yard of her hut are some shady, flat-topped acacia trees. Brightly colored yellow weaverbirds have made nests in the acacias. Every morning the birds chirp so loudly that they wake Asha up—just in time to enjoy the sunrise.

Asha's father, Salim, is a Moslem by faith and a fisherman by trade. He owns a small boat with a square sail; with a friend he goes out to the coral reefs to fish. He especially likes to catch red parrot fish, so called because they are red and have heads with parrotlike beaks. These sell for good

The women and girls of Asha's village carry jugs by balancing them on their heads.

Whenever Asha's family has surplus fruit, Asha brings it to the market to sell. *Above: Women wait for customers. Right: The people gather to talk and gossip. Below: Fruits and vegetables on display at the market.*

prices at the market because they are very tasty. Sometimes he catches lobsters, too. Salim has done well in his simple trade as a fisherman.

Over the years Salim has married three wives. This is acceptable and even encouraged by the Moslem faith. Asha's mother, a very attractive woman, is his first wife. She still wears the traditional grass skirts and is very industrious. While Salim fishes she looks after their little garden of corn, beans, tomatoes, and manioc (a starchy root). She didn't mind when Salim married the other two women, for she had the respect and household help of the two younger wives. Besides, these women were friends of hers and the three get along well together.

One of Asha's favorite dishes is made by boiling spinach leaves with fish meat; roasted green corn in the husk is also a favorite food. Everyone in Asha's family loves the juicy mangoes and the large papayas that grow in their garden. Whenever they have a surplus of mangoes or papayas, Asha carries them in a basket to the Kilifi market. Market is always fun— almost like a social event. The people gather to talk and gossip and bring all sorts of things to sell. Sometimes they just exchange, or barter, items instead of selling them. After Asha sells her fruit she usually stops at a *duka*, an Indian store, to buy whatever is needed at home. She buys such things as soap, kerosene for lamps, and sometimes rice to make the family meals more interesting.

Asha and her brothers and sisters often take short, adventurous trips into that mysterious-looking bushland just beyond the village. What could be hidden behind it all? Though she has heard many stories of wild animals, she has not seen many, except for little dikdik antelopes or guinea fowls that scoot under the bushes. She found out early, however, about the "wait-a-bit" thorns. These are found on certain bushes and have a way of hooking into a person and not letting go. No matter which way a person moves, the thorns hold. Very large, brown grasshoppers often fly up in the thornbush. Since Asha knows that these taste good when fried, she brings some home whenever she is able to catch them.

Asha does not expect to attend school. Most of the boys in her village attend school, but none of the girls do because they marry at a very young age.

One day there was much excitement in Kilifi. All the people were urged to go to the large playing field and listen to their great leader, the president himself. Asha went and heard the president talk about the free nation of Kenya and how important it was for everybody to pull together in "harambee" (togetherness) and build up their new nation.

That gave Asha a lot to think about. Maybe she would go to school after all and learn, and someday do great things for Kenya—but how? she wondered. It would not be easy to leave the life she loves at home.

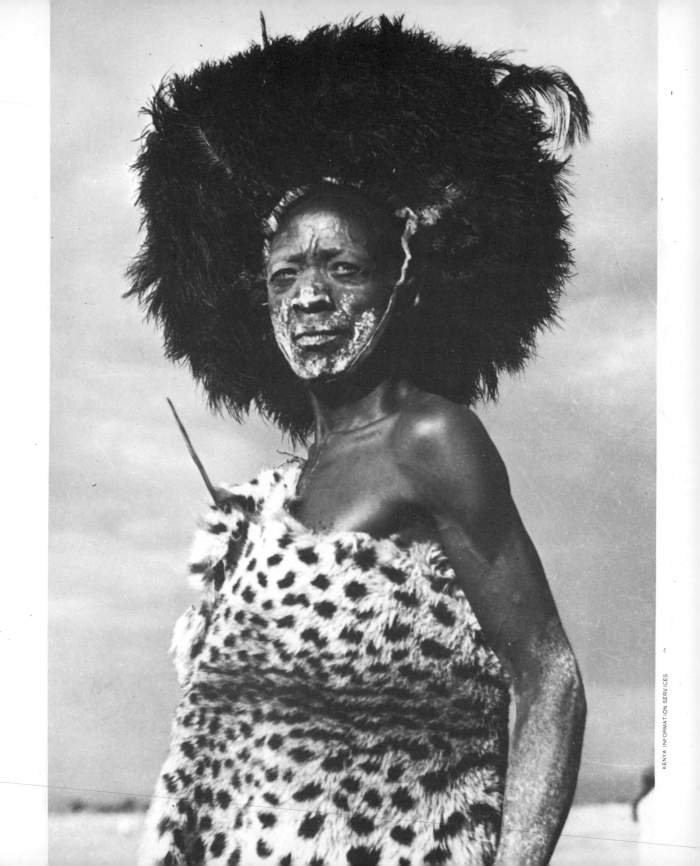

Kenya Yesterday

CRADLE OF MANKIND

Can it be that eastern Africa, rather than the Middle East, was the place where mankind originated? The late anthropologist-archaeologist Dr. L.S.B. Leakey seemed to think so. Discoveries made by Dr. Leakey and his wife in 1959 at Olorgasailie have been very startling. A skull of a prehistoric man, named *Zinjanthropus* by Dr. Leakey, indicates that man lived in the Kenya region two million years ago. After the Leakeys' discovery, another skull was found of a creature more manlike in appearance; he was named *Homo habilis*. It is known that this man fashioned and used stone tools.

According to Dr. Leakey's theories, man originated in the area of Kenya and then moved north, south, and west. The ones moving north became Caucasians and developed Semitic and Indo-European languages. Those who moved west were black and developed Niger-Congo languages; among these were the Bantu family of languages. Bushmen moved south and developed the Kloisan languages. Though there are many holes in Dr. Leakey's theories, the fossil he discovered is still one of the oldest fossils of man ever found.

Dr. Leakey's son Richard, a scientist in his own right, has been collaborating with American scientists. Recently Richard Leakey made interesting discoveries on the eastern shore of Lake Rudolf, where he found even more fossils and artifacts dating back about two million years. It is

Discoveries made by Dr. Leakey indicate that man lived in the Kenya region two million years ago.

31

Painstaking digging by Dr. Leakey and his wife was necessary in order to recover skull fragments of prehistoric man.

very likely that in time further discoveries will be made and will help to unravel some of the mysteries of early man in Kenya.

LONG-AGO VISITORS

Much more is known about the coast of eastern Africa than about its interior because the coast is more accessible.

It is very likely that the Assyrians and the Sumerians, two of the earliest civilizations, were the first to reach Kenya's coast. These people built ships and ventured forth on the high seas.

The Egyptians probably learned from the Sumerians how to build ships and soon they, too, were sailing down the coast. According to their writings and records, the Egyptians visited these regions as far back as 3,000 B.C. and traded with a land called Punt (believed to be present-day Somalia). From this part of the world came incense, spices, gold, ivory, and animal skins. Whether the Egyptians actually reached the coast of Kenya is not known.

Written records also tell of Phoenician traders who came to find gold and ivory for King Solomon. There are indications that they sailed along the coast as far as Mombasa and probably even as far south as Sofala on the Mozambique coast.

The Phoenicians, and possibly the early Jews, were great traders. According to the Bible, King Solomon and the Phoenician King Hiram collaborated in explorations and trade. These two kings sent their ships from the Red Sea port of Ezion-geber down the east coast of Africa to the land of Ophir (presumed to be the present-day Sofala). This took place about 1,000 B.C. Groups of Jews settled as far south as the Comoro Islands and Madagascar, and people in those islands had names such as Abraham, Lot, Moses, and Gideon. As these early Jews were not familiar with prophets who lived after the time of

Solomon, it appears that they may have arrived during the time of the alliance between King Solomon and King Hiram.

Later on came people from India, who made use of the monsoon winds to sail their ships to eastern Africa. They tried to establish small settlements along the coast; it is said that some even tried to penetrate farther into the interior and were perhaps among the first to reach the highlands.

Those visitors who had the most influence on the east coast were the Arabs. For at least three thousand years the history of eastern Africa was closely linked with that of the Arabs. These people took advantage of the monsoon winds and sailed regularly back and forth between Arabia and eastern Africa. At that time the African Bantu-speaking tribes also started migrating to the coast and considerable intermarriage took place between the early Arabs and Bantus. These people became the ancestors of the Swahili, whose language spread throughout eastern and central Africa to become the great *lingua franca* (common language) that it is today.

LONG-AGO INHABITANTS

What kind of people lived in the interior of Kenya long ago? Dr. Leakey gave us an inkling of prehistoric man, but the period before outside traders came is shrouded in mystery. There are no written records to help enlighten that part of ancient history, as there had been in the case of the coastal regions.

It appears that about three thousand years ago the inhabitants of Kenya's interior were Bushmen and hunters. From then on migrations came from the west, made up of peoples from the Niger-Congo areas; these peoples became the forerunners of the Bantus. From the north—Lower Egypt, Ethiopia, and possibly also Somalia—came the Nilo-Hamitic peoples. They divided into such groups as the Masai, Luo, and Nandi. Many of these peoples intermarried with other peoples and produced Bantu-speaking groups; examples are the Kikuyu, the Kamba, and the Chagga.

The short-statured Bushmen suffered a fate of almost total extermination by the invading peoples. Many Bushmen fled into the dense forests of what is now Zaire; others sought refuge in the waste of the Kalahari Desert in present-day Botswana. Intertribal warfare, especially between the northern tribes and the Bantus was quite common. Partly because the people moved around so much and were always forced to defend themselves against invaders, no permanent cities were built and no written language was developed. For these reasons, much of this early period is shrouded in mystery.

THE PORTUGUESE ERA

For hundreds of years, from A.D. 975 to A.D. 1497, various Arab sultans vied, or rivaled each other, for influence and power in eastern Africa, establishing what was known as the Zenj Empire. The island of Zanzibar off the coast of Tanzania became an important focal point of Arab dominion over the coast.

The Zenj Empire was brought to an end by the coming of the Portuguese. These people were the first to come to Africa from Europe; the well-known Portuguese explorer Vasco da Gama figures prominently in establishing Portuguese influence and power along the east coast of Africa. In the small Kenyan port of Malindi is an old monument built in honor of Vasco da Gama. In the year 1498 this fearless explorer, who had sailed from Portugal, rounded the southern tip of Africa and sailed north along the east coast, visiting Mombasa and Malindi. He visited India as well, stopping to trade there for about a year, then sailed back to Malindi. Having opened the route for the Portuguese, Vasco da Gama made several other trips. More ships arrived and the years 1500 to 1509 were years of conquest and defeat of the Arabs.

In 1593 the Portuguese built a fort on the island of Mombasa called Fort Jesus. This fort still stands, looking out across the Indian Ocean. Now, however, it is a museum designed to describe Portuguese conquest and glory.

ARABS REGAIN POWER

The Portuguese period of domination lasted until 1741, when the Mazrui Arab clan living in Mombasa grew in strength and finally ousted the Portuguese from that city. Then came the powerful Sultan of Oman, Seyyid Said, who defeated the Mazrui clan and established himself as ruler in 1832. He made the island of Zanzibar his capital and ruled until his death in 1856. Seyyid Said introduced the planting of clove trees; this spice became and still is Zanzibar's main export.

Americans first arrived in eastern Africa during the reign of Seyyid Said. They established an American consulate in Zanzibar in 1837. The British followed, and in 1841 also established a consulate there.

BEGINNINGS OF EUROPEAN INFLUENCE

During the second half of the nineteenth century, Europe began to increase its trade with Africa. A gradual penetration into the interior took place, and certain portions of Africa were claimed by European powers as "spheres of influence," large areas where no other European power was supposed to interfere or colonize.

Reports by the British explorer Dr. David Livingstone concerning the horrible conditions of the slave trade brought strong action by Great Britain against this trade. Livingstone published a book on his explorations; this report on conditions in Africa drew all types of men to Africa. Many of these were missionaries. In

Sailors mend a sail near Fort Jesus on the Indian Ocean.

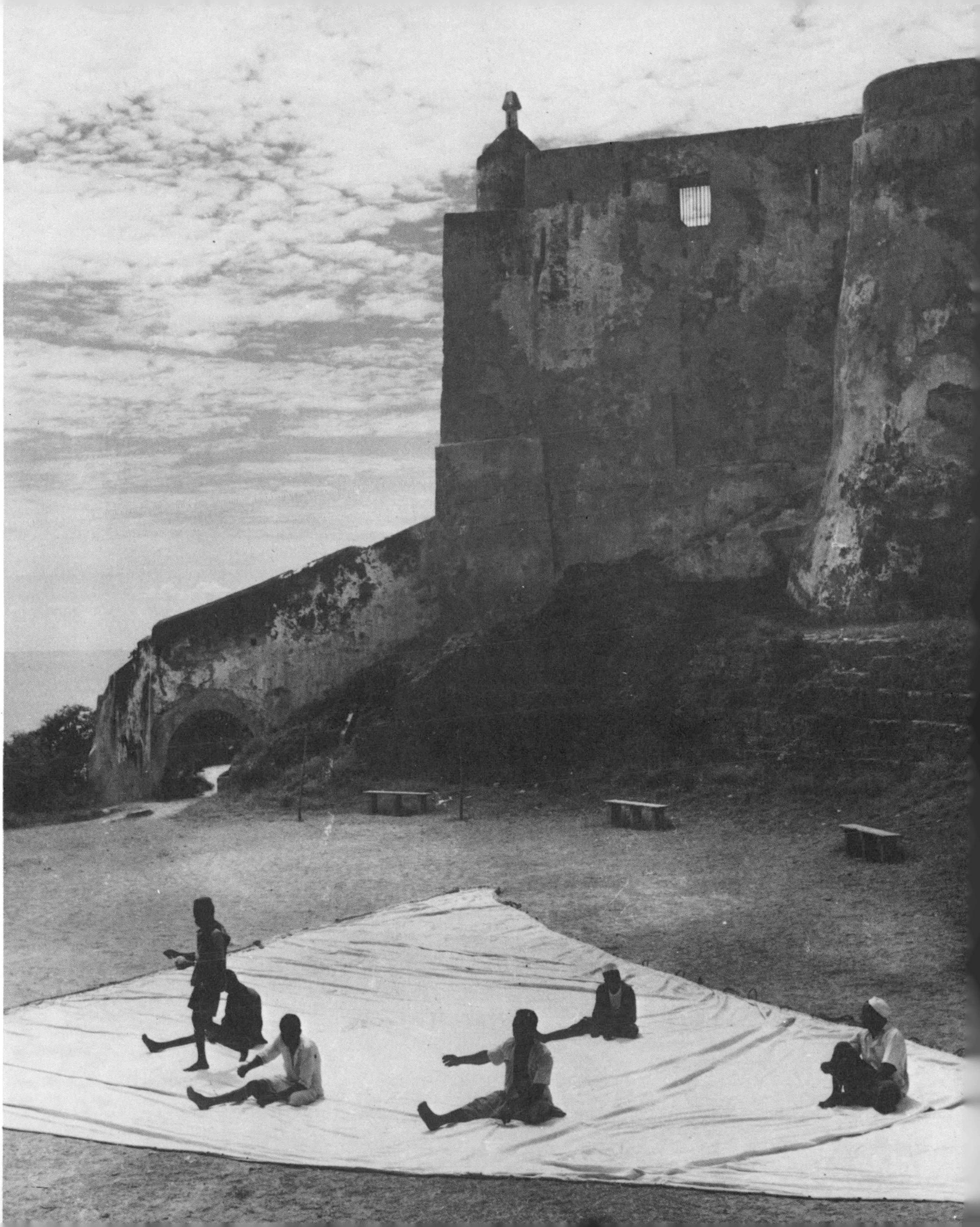
KENYA INFORMATION SERVICES

Kenya the great missionary pioneers were Dr. J. L. Krapf, Johann Rebmann, Bishop Steere, and Bishop Hannington (who was murdered during his stay in the interior of Uganda). Besides trying to convert the people to Christianity, these men studied the Swahili language, produced dictionaries and grammars of it, translated portions of the Bible into it, and laid foundations for others to continue in their work.

KENYA BECOMES BRITISH

Many important events took place toward the end of the nineteenth century that opened up eastern Africa for European colonists. One of these was the 1869 opening of the Suez Canal, which linked the Mediterranean and Red seas through Egypt. The canal gave European ships a short, convenient route to eastern Africa; they no longer had to travel around the Cape of Good Hope and come back up the Indian Ocean side. Three years after the canal was opened, the British India Steam Navigation Company started a monthly service between Aden in the Middle East and Zanzibar. In 1879 the Eastern Telegraph Company completed an undersea cable between Aden and Zanzibar, bringing the African coast even closer to the outside world.

The Suez Canal helped to link the Middle East with eastern Africa. Even today, Arab dhows *(boats) can be seen in the old harbor at Mombasa.*

Construction of the railroad was a difficult task. Today railroads link Kenya's cities.

In 1888 the British formed the Imperial British East Africa Company. This organization tried to gain control over parts of Kenya and Uganda but soon went out of business. The British government was forced to assume control of these areas. Kenya and Uganda became an integral part of the British Empire in 1895.

THE KENYA-UGANDA RAILWAY

The first major task the British undertook in eastern Africa was to start building a railroad from Mombasa north to Lake Victoria; this was a difficult project. The line had to climb from Mombasa on the coast all the way up the highlands to an altitude of seven thousand feet, drop about five thousand feet into the Rift Valley, then climb right up again on the other side of the Rift to about nine thousand feet before it descended once again to Lake Victoria. Geographical features were not the only obstacle—there were labor problems, too, such as the man-eating lions at Tsavo which held up construction for months, and a shortage of skilled workers. Some thirty-two thousand workers were imported from India because local labor was not skilled at that time, nor was it readily available. These Indians became the nucleus for Indian settlement in eastern Africa.

37

In the early 1900s, many British settlers came to Kenya. Most of them became farmers in the highlands. Today one-third of the people in Kenya are farmers.

It was not until 1899 that the place where Nairobi is now located was reached. The small settlement that was there grew during construction of the railroad across the Rift Valley. In 1901 the railroad finally reached the port of Kisumu on Lake Victoria. It had taken six long years to reach that point, but the completion was a great accomplishment.

KENYA ATTRACTS SETTLERS

With the railroad completed as far as Lake Victoria, British settlers started coming into Kenya in very large numbers. Among them was the great pioneer, Lord Delamere. Until that time the highlands had been largely unoccupied. Both Delamere and his son did much to help the settlers, most of whom became farmers in the beautiful highlands. The Kenya National Farmers' Union was organized, and in years to come, most of the farmers depended on it in marketing their products.

World War I was not remote to those living in Kenya. Next-door Tanganyika was a German colony, and it was not long before fighting flared up even there. Most of Kenya's British immigrants enlisted and did their share of fighting. There were also battalions of African native troops, since at that time the British armed forces were not integrated. When Germany was defeated (in Europe), Tanganyika became a British Mandated Territory; after that, it drew closer to Kenya.

A COLONY FORGES AHEAD

The British settlers, having fought to keep Kenya British, were now even more intent on making it their permanent home. The proclamation of Kenya as a Crown Colony in 1920 seemed to clinch the matter. A legislative council was set up and soon the first elections for it were held.

The new capital of Nairobi grew. Because many new townships developed along the railroad, branch lines had to be added to accommodate them. Some of the new settlements were Nakuru, in the Rift Valley; Nyeri, on the slopes of Mount Kenya; Kisumu, the port on Lake Victoria; and Eldoret and Kitale, north of Nakuru.

In colonial times the title of the present Republic of Kenya was "Kenya Colony and Protectorate." The name Protectorate referred to a ten-mile-wide strip of the coastline of Kenya which had been claimed by the sultan of Zanzibar. This strip was leased and administered by the British government.

AFRICANS LEARN

During all of this time missionaries from established Christian churches were also very active. Aside from their obvious concern with spreading Christianity, especially among the native Africans, they were also concerned with medical work and with establishing schools. They trained teachers and established many primary schools and later some secondary schools for Africans.

It was only natural that native Africans were more and more concerned about their own position. They saw the powers of government and other rights in the hands of the white settlers, while they had few rights or powers. Many Africans had been educated and others had served as soldiers during World War I; now they, too, wanted a voice in government. Because the British Colonial Office was in favor of this, in 1922 it proposed that a list of voters (called the Common Roll) be made up of both Africans and settlers. Settlers refused this in 1923, saying that the Colonial Office was too far away to understand their views of the situation. A compromise was reached later in 1923. The British declared that Kenya would be held in trust for the Africans until it was felt that they were able to make their own political decisions.

As happened in other areas of Africa, Kenya's settlers had long felt that they should be united with their neighbors in other territories. In 1927 the government tried to make a union of Kenya, Uganda, and Tanganyika. Indians and Africans opposed this union, however, and made their feelings known. The proposed union never took place. Years later, in 1948, the East African High Commission was created; this agency was set up so that the three east African nations could work together on mutual concerns.

WORLD WAR II

When World War II broke out Kenya was again involved. This time the fighting was directed against the Italians who had occupied Ethiopia. In Kenya were kept large numbers of Italian prisoners of war, many of whom worked either on farms or in industry; one group worked on paving the main road from Nairobi to Kisumu. As in the previous war, many of the settlers and a large number of African troops served—not only against the Italians in Ethiopia, but also in the Middle East and against the Japanese in Burma.

Not until 1944 was the first African nominated to the legislative council. This was the first step toward the Africans' goal of having a say in the matters of their government. It would be thirteen more years, however, before a new constitution would be adopted making the council truly multiracial.

Both during and shortly after World War II, fear continued to increase among the Africans that the white settlers were becoming too strong in matters of government. Desire among Africans for land was growing greater but so was unemployment, especially in the cities. Africans began to feel that they would lose what little they had if they did not take some strong action.

MAU MAU

As early as 1948, a secret terrorist society called the Mau Mau was known to

During the Mau Mau terror, a state of emergency was declared by the government.

exist. This group wanted to expel European settlers for what seemed to be nationalistic reasons. Membership in the Mau Mau was made up of the Kikuyu, the largest African group in Kenya, and the smaller Embu and Mweru groups. By 1950 the organization was banned and in 1952 a state of emergency due to Mau Mau activity was declared by the government. The height of Mau Mau activity took place from 1952 to 1956, though it was not until 1960 that the Mau Mau were felt to be under control. The so-called leader of the Mau Mau, Jomo Kenyatta, was put in detention in 1952 and the Kenya African Union (KAU) political party, founded in 1946, was banned because of its supposed relationship with the Mau Mau.

During the Mau Mau terror, 2,356 Africans loyal to the government were killed. Of these only 524 were members of the se-

41

curity forces. Only 32 European residents were killed, along with 63 soldiers of the European security force.

CHANGES AND POLITICAL GAINS

In 1957 a new constitution went into effect. It was called the Lennox-Boyd Constitution, after the man who was instrumental in writing it. This constitution gave Africans equal right to representation in government. Soon after, the first Africans were elected to the legislative council. National political parties were permitted in July, 1959, but only if they declared themselves to be multiracial. The Kikuyu and the Luo together organized a national party, the Kenya African National Union (KANU). This was by far the most power-ful and largest party because the two tribes were the largest in Kenya. Jomo Kenyatta was chosen as the leader, but the British government did not approve because of Kenyatta's previous record of alleged association with the Mau Mau. The party temporarily elected James Gichuru acting president until Jomo Kenyatta was cleared in 1961. Oginga Odinga was then chosen as vice-president and Tom Mboya as secretary.

The opposition party was the Kenya African Democratic Union (KADU), led by Ronald Ngala and Masinde Muliro. This party represented an alliance between the coastal tribes, the Masai, the Kalenjin, and some Luhya parties. It was not as large and powerful as KANU, but it was, nevertheless, the opposition party.

Jomo Kenyatta became leader of the KANU in 1961, after being cleared of his alleged association with the Mau Mau. When the country gained its independence from Britain in 1964, he became president.

AFRICAPIX

Kenya Today

UHURU!

Independence finally came to Kenya on December 12, 1963. The Swahili cry "Uhuru!" (freedom) rang through the land. This was truly a great day for all Africans in Kenya, for the British flag was lowered and the new flag was raised. The Kenyan flag had three stripes—black, red, and green—separated by two bands of white, with a warrior's shield and crossed spears in the center.

At this time Kenya became an independent member of the British Commonwealth of Nations. It was to be governed by a freely elected parliament and a prime minister, but would have a British governor-general (as a link to the British government).

On December 12, 1964, one year after independence, Kenya became a republic within the Commonwealth and Jomo Kenyatta, leader of KANU, became president. The rallying cry of President Kenyatta, or *Mzee* Kenyatta (Grand Old Man) as he is affectionately called, was the Swahili word "harambee," which means togetherness—all races and peoples, tribes and religions, were urged to unite under the flag of Kenya and cooperate with each other in pulling together to make the new nation succeed. Under the constitution Kenya is declared a sovereign republic, one that provides for the protection of the rights and freedoms of all its citizens. The president is both head of state and commander in chief of the armed forces. He is assisted by a cabinet of ministers whom he appoints from members of Parliament. The Parliament consists of a single chamber called the National Assembly, with 158 elected members. The executive and legislative powers of the constitution are divided in

Upon receiving self-government, Kenyatta dedicated his country to complete independence from any foreign domination. Above: To commemorate self-government, "Madaraka Day" is observed as a day for remembering and rejoicing in freedom. Below: The State Opening of the National Assembly by President Kenyatta in February, 1967.

order to support three main principles: strong national leadership is to exist and be so recognized by the people; the president and his cabinet are to be responsible to Parliament; and Parliament is to have final lawmaking powers.

TRIBALISM

In order to achieve better national unity in Kenya, the problem of tribalism must be solved. There are forty main ethnic groups in Kenya, each with its own language, culture, and customs. Some of these tribes have always been enemies. Kenyatta's rallying cry of "harambee!" emphasized that all people were to think of themselves as *Kenyans,* rather than as members of a certain group.

It has not been easy to achieve the kind of national unity expressed in the slogan "harambee!" For example, the Kikuyu (a Bantu tribe) and the Luo (a Nilotic tribe) have long competed for leadership both in politics and in the marketplace. In 1969 Tom Mboya, a Luo who was Minister of Economic Planning and Development and a possible candidate for the presidency in the next general elections, was assassinated. Though the reasons for the assassination are not clear, it caused much bitterness among the Luo.

LAND

Under the new constitution land reforms assumed great importance. The European settlers had owned huge chunks of land for their farms. Now large acreages of land owned by settlers were bought by the government and given in small parcels to Africans who had no land. All native-owned land came under the heading of "trust lands"— control of them was taken over by the government. Most native-owned land was held by the different tribes or clans. Each man was given a certain amount of land on which to work. Traditionally, it was very important that each person had some land of his own, whether he farmed on it or not. Kenyans practiced *land fragmentation*, the process of dividing one's land among one's sons. For example, a ten-acre piece of land would be divided by a father among his five sons to give each son only two acres. The process would continue through each generation. These sons would divide their land among their own sons, and so on until there was not enough land left to divide.

Today the government is trying to stop land fragmentation. Title deeds have been issued for the possession of a piece of land. Those who cannot get land in their home areas have to move elsewhere. Eventually all the land will be owned and many people will be forced to move to the cities, earning their livings from jobs there.

EDUCATION

The growth of schools since independence has been phenomenal. By 1970 there were about 6,200 primary schools

The growth of schools since independence has been phenomenal.
Today 30 percent of the people in Kenya can read and write.

with an approximate enrollment of 120,000 pupils. Teachers are urgently needed to staff all these schools. The twenty-four teacher training colleges in Kenya are kept busy instructing teachers; more than six thousand teachers are graduated each year.

The national radio is used extensively to broadcast to schools, using special programs that are prepared for that purpose. In one year 780 such programs were on the air. The University of Nairobi also operates a radio correspondence course for adults.

So far the University of Nairobi is the only university in Kenya. About 280 professors are on the university staff and the enrollment of students is more than two thousand. The hunger for higher education is great and about forty-five hundred students attend colleges and universities in other countries. Of these, about seven hundred study in the United States and nearly two thousand study in the United Kingdom.

Other schools include the Kenya Polytechnic Institute in Nairobi and the Technical Institute in Mombasa. These schools provide technical and vocational training, graduating students with the skills so necessary in a new and growing country.

CONTEMPORARY CHALLENGES

Along with the expansion of the educational system, another challenge for Kenya is expansion of the medical system. Urban areas have government hospitals, along with mission and private hospitals. In rural areas dispensaries and health care centers do as much of the work as they can, not only in curing disease but also in preventive medicine.

Research continues in combating diseases such as malaria, sleeping sickness, and amoebic dysentery. With the aid of the United Nations World Health Organization (WHO), students at the University of Nairobi medical school are trained in medicine. Later many of these students go to medical schools overseas to become doctors.

Kenya joined the Space Age in 1971. Through a joint venture of the United States and Italy, a satellite that would study the ionosphere was launched from Malindi on the Indian Ocean.

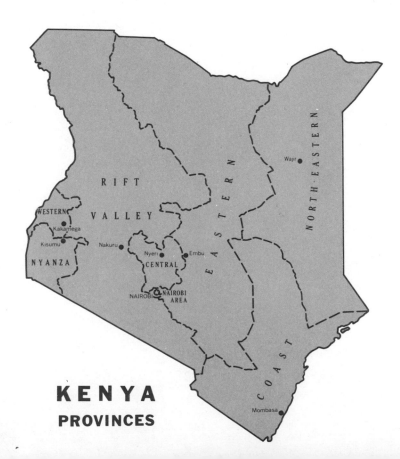

RIFT VALLEY

WESTERN
Kakamega

Kisumu
Nakuru
NYANZA
Nyeri
Embu
CENTRAL

EASTERN

NORTH-EASTERN

Wajir

NAIROBI
NAIROBI AREA

COAST

Mombasa

KENYA
PROVINCES

Natural Treasures

ANIMALS

The government and most of the residents of Kenya realize that many species of wild animals living in Kenya are a real treasure. Poaching, illegal killing of the animals, has always been a problem. By setting aside national parks and game parks, an attempt is made to preserve this treasure, but even there poachers sometimes intrude.

The most important of the *pachyderms,* hoofed mammals that have thick skins, is the African elephant. It is somewhat larger in size and not as easily domesticated as the Indian elephant. Though elephants are usually seen in small groups, they are sometimes found in very large herds. For centuries African elephants have been hunted for the valuable treasure of ivory supplied by their tusks.

The rhinoceros, also a pachyderm, is an unpredictable creature that can crash through the bushland at great speeds, even though it weighs more than two tons. The Swahili name for the rhinoceros, *kifaru,* is also the name given to an armored war tank because of its ability to crash through the bush as the rhinoceros does.

Another thick-skinned animal, though not a pachyderm, is the hippopotamus. It spends most of its time in lakes and rivers, but at night goes out on land to search for food. The elephant, the rhi-

A rhinoceros near Mount Kenya. One of the largest land creatures, the rhinoceros is harmless unless provoked. Usually it will run to safety, but if wounded or confused, it may charge. For a short distance, it can run as fast as a horse.

KENYA INFORMATION SERVICES

A baby giraffe follows its mother. Giraffes are a common sight in the bushland of Kenya.

noceros, and the hippopotamus are vegetarians—they do not eat meat. The hippopotamus, like the rhinoceros, weighs more than two tons.

Driving through the game parks or even on the highways, one often comes across a group of giraffes near the road. They are the tallest animals in Africa—some reach eighteen feet. They look curiously at cars as they pass. Because of their long legs, their manner of running appears very awkward. In spite of the long neck, to drink water the giraffe still must stretch its front legs apart in order to reach ground level with its mouth.

Perhaps one of the most cunning and dangerous of the big game animals is the African, or black, buffalo. If wounded, it often comes back to the path of the hunter and waits there to seek revenge. The buffalo is a massive creature weighing three quarters of a ton. It should not be confused with the Asian water buffalo,

which does not exist in Africa. Though the water buffalo can be tamed, or domesticated, the African buffalo cannot.

There are many species of antelope in Kenya, varying greatly in size. Some are the size of large elk and some are tiny creatures fifteen inches high that weigh only twelve pounds. Among the larger species of antelope are the kudu with its beautiful spiral horns, and the eland, perhaps the largest and heaviest of the antelopes. The sable antelope found in the Shimba Hills near Mombasa is magnificent with its curved horns; equally attractive is the oryx with its long, straight horns. The impala is a fleet-footed, graceful animal that can clear thirty feet in a jump. The waterbuck is large and somewhat long-haired; it likes to browse near water, which is how it gets its name. A very common, but ungainly, antelope is the hartebeest or *kongoni*. The hartebeest can be found almost everywhere in lowland regions, usually in large herds together with zebras and gnus. The gnu's head looks like that of a small buffalo, yet its build is more like that of an antelope.

Also in the antelope family are the Grant's and Thomson's gazelles. These are smallish animals, about the size of goats, yet very graceful and attractive. They are found in large groups on the Athi plains outside of Nairobi.

The forest, too, has its specialties and among them is the bongo, a beautiful reddish-colored antelope with stripes. A very shy animal, the bongo is seldom seen. Another smallish antelope that looks peculiar because of its long neck and giraffelike head is the gerenuk. It often stands on its hind legs nibbling at soft shoots of tall bushes. Finally, the very smallest antelopes are the tiny dikdiks. They live in pairs and can survive even in very dry country; many Kenyans keep them as pets.

The well-known zebra is numerous in Kenya and lives in large herds on the plains. The different varieties of zebras

The zebra's stripes blend with the background, hiding the zebra from its enemies.

Large cats such as leopards and lions roam Kenya's grasslands. Lions (right) live in groups called prides; each pride stays in a certain territory. The male guards the territory while the female hunts for food. Leopards (below) are quite strong and are good climbers. Sometimes a leopard will carry an animal that it has killed into a tree to eat it.

Lively monkey in Nairobi National Park. Some kinds of monkeys spend their entire lives in trees, swinging from branches, while others roam on the ground.

can be told apart by their striping pattern. Because of their bright, clean-looking black and white stripes, they give the appearance of being especially healthy and lively.

Lively monkeys, including some that like to mock human beings, are found in most parts of Kenya. The large baboons travel in groups, or colonies; if they can get into a garden to clean out the corn crop, they will surely do so. In Nairobi National Park baboons sometimes jump on the hood or roof of a car, then stare insolently at the driver.

The most attractive of the monkeys are the colobi, which live in the trees of Kenya's forests. Unfortunately, the colobi are hunted for their unusual and very attractive skins—black with long, white shoulder capes and white, bushy tails. These skins are often used as special outfits by chiefs or ceremonial dancers.

There is a real danger that these gentle monkeys, who add so much to the charm of the Kenya forests, may die out if not protected.

There are also several smaller varieties of gray vervet and other blue monkeys; these are very lively and spend their time both on the ground and in the trees. Finally, a tiny lemur called the "bush baby" is perhaps the most charming of the monkeys. It is so tiny that it can fit into a man's coat pocket, and it makes an adorable pet.

Among the *carnivores*, animals that eat meat, the regal lions are the most important, followed by the cunning leopard, then the fleet-footed cheetah. The leopard is ruthlessly hunted because of its valuable and beautiful skin. Kenya's government must take steps to protect this treasure.

Packs of wild dogs are prevalent in some areas of the country. They can be dangerous because they hunt down their quarry with much cunning. The hyena and the jackal, also carnivores, are actually more like scavengers. Together with the vultures they clean up all carcasses left on the plains—a perfect example of natural ecology at work.

BIRDS AND FISH

Kenya is a true paradise for birds of many species. Among the exotic birds found in Kenya is the ostrich—a bird that cannot fly. Its lack of flying ability is due to its size; it may stand nearly eight feet tall. The ostrich can run fast, however, attaining speeds of up to forty-five miles per hour. It can also defend itself with its strong legs; a hard kick from an ostrich could kill a man.

Colorful pink flamingos congregate and breed in groups of thousands at Lake Nakuru. Herons and other water birds such as ducks and geese stop there, too. Elsewhere, storks can be seen seasonally on their migrations between South Africa and Europe. Perhaps the most interesting is the heavy-set marabou stork whose very fine, fluffy undertail feathers were once greatly prized as trim for fancy hats. Circling high above in the sky are various kinds of sharp-eyed eagles, hawks, and vultures.

In the bushland it is quite common to observe guinea fowl and partridges scooting here and there in the underbush. Pigeons sit in the small trees cooing their mournful song. A peculiar call signals that a honey bird wants help in getting at the honey in a bees' nest in some tree hollow.

Trout in the mountain streams, talapia in the lakes, and a variety of fine fish in the ocean off the coast all contribute to Kenya's wealth. Among the saltwater fish are swordfish, barracuda, dolphin, and parrot fish.

PLANTS

Woods and Trees   The forests in the highlands and on the slopes of high mountains such as Mount Kenya abound in varieties of good timber: wild red cedar, which grows on the edges of the Rift Valley; podocarpus, a type of evergreen that provides good building material; and types of mahogany and other trees that are not only attractive to look at but provide good hardwoods. Among the rarer of the hardwoods is the huge but slow-growing tree called *mvule*. It is a favorite of furniture craftsmen because of its attractive fine grain and color. Acacia and wattle trees grow naturally in the highlands and are now cultivated. From the bark of the wattle a good quality tannin (used for making leather and ink) is extracted. The poles and slim stems of the wattles are also a favorite for building huts.

The baobab is a good example of an exotic tree. These trees grow in hotter climates and are not very tall. They look even stubbier because of their very wide trunks—so wide that it sometimes takes up to thirty people joining hands to encircle such a tree.

Kenya is truly a bird paradise. Storks, such as the marabou (left), a bird with beautiful white feathers, stop here on their migrations between South Africa and Europe. Ostriches (below) roam the plains along with elands and other wild animals.

Along the coast in brackish inlets grow the peculiar mangrove trees, with their roots right in the salt water. The slim, straight poles and trunks are used for building huts along the coast.

The adept woodcarvers of Kenya often carve their figurines from wild olive, which is very hard, has an attractive grain, and will take a high polish. They also use wood from the rare ebony tree. Though the ebony tree grows wild in the plains, it is not a large tree and is often stunted in its growth by prairie fires; this accounts for the rarity of its wood. Ebony is perhaps the hardest wood known.

Trees of the euphorbia family come in many varieties, from the small Christ's-thorn to the large, exotic evergreen tree called the candelabra euphorbia. This particular tree stands out, for even in the driest seasons when everything else looks dead and brown, it remains green. Its many candelabralike branches reach up to heights of more than twenty feet. The candelabra euphorbia seems to stand as a sentinel of some prehistoric age.

Flowers   It has been truly said that Kenya is also a land of flowers and gardens. There are many beautiful indigenous flowers such as the climbing begonias seen on forest trees; gladioli and heather found in high-altitude, Alpine-like meadows; varieties of orchids; the pink Cape chestnut; orange aloes; and blue pentas that burst into bloom for a while. Hundreds of flowers, flowering bushes, and trees have been imported over the years from many parts of the world. Many of these have adapted so well that they grow in semiwild states. Others flourish in the thousands of well-planned gardens in Nairobi's residential areas and parks, and

Wood from wild olive and ebony trees is used for carving figurines of animals.

This gold mine at Migori began production in 1966.

in many other towns of Kenya. The British settlers were garden lovers and everywhere they went gardens were laid out.

Outstanding for their lavish colors are the jacaranda tree with its gorgeous plumes of lilac blue; the red flamboyant with feathery leaves, found mostly in the warmer climates; and the ever-present bougainvillea climber which is now grown in different colors. To add to the color and beauty of the flowers both in nature and in the gardens, thousands of colorful insects flit to and fro seeking their nectar, as do flashy and iridescent-colored humming-birds or colibri.

MINERALS

At the present time not much is known about the treasures buried deep in Kenya's earth. There have been no spectacular finds so far, though people are looking, especially for oil. Near Kakamega some gold and copper has been found. *Diatomite,* fossilized skeletons of tiny algae, is mined in the Rift Valley near Nakuru. These mines are somewhat productive. At this time, however, Kenya's main mineral resource lies around Lake Magadi, where thousands of tons of salt and soda are mined.

People Live in Kenya

AFRICAN ANCESTRY

Modern Kenya's population is overwhelmingly African, though this general group is made up of many different races and native tribes.

There are forty main ethnic groups and about thirty subgroups living in Kenya. These can be divided into three main categories: Bantu, Nilotic, and Cushitic.

Bantu These tribes live mainly on the coast, though some live in western Kenya. In Central Province live quite a large group of Bantu speakers, including the Kikuyu, the largest and most influential tribe in Kenya. Other Central Province Bantus are the Embu, Mweru, Mbere, and Thakara. Elsewhere in Kenya are the Swahili, with seven subgroups; the Talta, with three subgroups; and the Luhya, with sixteen subgroups. Other Bantus include the Kisii and the Kuria, two smaller tribes near the Tanzanian border, and the Pokomo tribe on the Tana River. The Kamba are located southeast of Nairobi; most of Kenya's loyal soldiers come from this group.

Nilotic In this group the Luo, who live near Lake Victoria, are by far the largest tribe. Since they are the second largest tribe in Kenya, they give considerable competition to the Kikuyu. The Elgeyo, Marakwet, and Nandi live on the high plateau around Eldoret, and farther

A young African girl of Kenya. Most women and girls wear simple clothing and are adorned with necklaces and earrings.

These Masai women are selling African items in a market.

out still live the Suk, Terik, and Sabaot. The Kipsigis tribe lives in the tea-growing area around Kericho. Nomadic people of this language group, who still have large herds of cattle and like to roam the ranges in the plains, include the Masai, Samburu, Turkana, and Teso. Another tribe, the Ndorobo, is scattered throughout the Rift Valley.

Cushitic (Somali) These are tribes that have come over from Somalia and southern Ethiopia, and perhaps even from the Sudan. The Cushitic people live in the semiarid regions of north and northeastern Kenya. The Somali-speaking group is extremely large, numbering over 275,000. Some people in Somalia would like to annex northeast Kenya because they feel a kinship with Kenya's Somali-speaking residents. The other tribes of the Cushitic group are fairly small and are scattered across the northern regions from around Lake Rudolf to the east and south as far as the Tana River. These tribes are the Rendille, Galla, Boran, Gabra, Orma, Marille, Gosha, Langulu, Boni, Sanye, and Dahalo.

It is important to understand that each of these ethnic groups thinks of its own group as a separate unit, rather than as a group of people who are part of a larger nation. Through education, radio, and emphasis on travel, the government is doing its utmost to unify all these people in the spirit of "harambee!" Mzee Jomo Kenyatta has stressed this idea of togetherness repeatedly when talking to his people. On one occasion Kenyatta stated, "Beware of negative belligerent tribalism that sees no good in an alien tribe. It must go! Forget that your origin is Kikuyu, Kipsigis, Suk, Luo, or any other tribe. Substitute your tribalism with mass nationalism—unity. *Uhuru na Umoja!*" The Swahili words at the end of this quote mean "freedom and unity" in English and could be considered the "national motto" of Kenya. The government of Kenya is hopeful that the problem of national unity will soon be solved.

OTHER KENYANS

Asians   Most of the people known as Asians are actually immigrants from India. At the turn of the century when the railway was being built from Mombasa to Nairobi, a great number of workers were brought over from India to help. Most of these people stayed in Kenya when the railroad was completed, hoping to find a new home there. Many more came later from India, for both India and Kenya were under the flag of the British Empire.

These Indians did not find life easy in their newly adopted country. The government did not permit them to own land, develop farms in the highlands as the Europeans did, or participate in similar enterprises. One of the few opportunities left open to them was trade and business. It was not long before *dukas,* small Indian-owned shops, appeared in most of Kenya's communities and townships. The dukas served a good purpose. People of all races learned to rely on them for groceries, kerosene, soap, small farm tools, blankets, cloth, and many other items. Their trade grew and many Indian businessmen became quite prosperous.

Not only in trade and business were they successful, but also in office work, especially in government offices as clerks and accountants, in banks, in post offices, and in the crafts as tailors, shoemakers, and carpenters; most of the stationmasters on the railway line were Indians. At its peak, the population of the Indian community in Kenya was 190,000.

PHOTOS ON THESE PAGES COURTESY OF KENYA INFORMATION SERVICES

Above: The tall, thin Masai people live in southern Kenya. Right: Masai girl. Below: Masai girls getting ready for a ceremony.

The many tribes of Kenya each have their
own culture. Left: This old African man
has large holes in his ears because he
has worn earrings for so many years.
Above: A group performs a traditional
dance. Below: A group of warriors.

Many Indians and Arabs have small businesses or shops like this one.

After independence the government of Kenya gave all non-Africans—Asians and Europeans alike—the opportunity to become citizens of Kenya. The British government had told the Indians earlier that they could also choose British citizenship, and about half of the Indian population chose to have a British passport. The government had set up a two-year period of grace in which noncitizens could remain in their existing jobs. After the two-year period, all non-Africans who had not taken out Kenyan citizenship had to give up their jobs and businesses so that citizens could take over. Consequently, about one hundred thousand Indians who had chosen British citizenship were forced to leave. Some returned to India but most wished to go to Great Britain. The number of Indians wishing to enter Britain from Kenya was so large that the British government had to limit the number it would accept. Because many Indians were stranded, there was much bitterness.

Europeans   After independence a great period of readjustment came to the Europeans, too. They were no longer members of the ruling nation of Kenya. Many who found this difficult to accept sold their businesses and left Kenya. The majority, however, accepted the change, tried to fit in, and became citizens.

Since independence some new European immigrants have come to Kenya, and there are now about fifty thousand Europeans living there. Some of these people are government officials from other nations who are serving as representatives in various government services or embassies. Since most of these people live in Nairobi, the city has become a large international metropolis. Missionaries, both Protestant and Roman Catholic, also live and work in Kenya, but mostly in rural areas. There are a great number of American missionaries in Kenya.

A large number of Arabs have lived along the east coast for as long as anyone can remember. Most of them have small businesses, shops, or farms, where they grow coconuts and tropical fruits such as mangoes, guavas, bananas, papayas, and cashew nuts. A few enterprising Indians and Europeans have joined them. Quite a few of the Arab men have married native African women. There are now about forty thousand Arabs living in Kenya.

THE FAITH OF THE PEOPLE

With the great diversity of races and tribes in Kenya, it is only natural that there would also be a diversity of religious beliefs and customs.

Christianity Christian missionaries first came to Kenya in 1844, beginning their work at the coast near Mombasa. Venturing into the interior through Kamba and Kikuyu country, the missionaries went as far as Lake Victoria. By the early 1860s more than half of the African population was considered to be Christian. The activities of the Roman Catholic Church and the Protestant denominations are co-ordinated through the Christian Council of Kenya, which also controls the large educational program of the missions.

Eastern Religions Islam, the Moslem faith, came to Kenya very early in its history, when Arabs occupied the coastal regions. Islam is still strong along the coast, and today it is also well established in the Somali-speaking groups of northeast Kenya. There are Moslem communities in most urban areas and there are two large *mosques* (houses of worship) in Nairobi. Some of the Asians who originally came from what is now Pakistan and Bangladesh are Moslems.

In the Asian community a large number practice Hinduism. This religion is based on a collection of various traditions and cults. One of these traditions is the *caste system*; each individual is a member of a definite social class, or *caste*. A person's caste is determined by his parents' caste, and one's caste can never be altered during one's lifetime. The castes range from the *Brahmins,* the aristocratic class, down to the *Untouchables,* the lowest caste of all.

The Sikhs are also a distinctive community of Asians. Their religious practices resemble Christianity more than do those of the Hindus. The Sikhs have regular services on Sundays, while the Moslem day of worship is Friday.

Animism Those Africans who are neither Christian nor Moslem practice various forms of *animism*. They believe that every natural object, every natural phenomenon, and even the universe itself possesses a soul, or spirit. Many of these spirits must be worshipped or appeased. Ancestor worship is extremely important to believers of animism.

MUSIC

Basic to African music are drums of various types and sizes. These drums are hollowed-out sections of tree trunks over which skin is stretched. Very often the skin of the zebra is used. A popular instrument is the *mbira,* the size of a small box with a series of metal strips fitted on it in such a way that the strips can be tuned and then plucked. Various types of flutes and horns are used as wind instruments, played alone or with drums. Instruments similar to the xylophone can also be found in Kenya, but more common are certain types of string instruments.

All these older types of musical instruments are used mostly with ceremonial and traditional dances and songs. The most popular modern instrument is the guitar. Popular songs in Swahili are accompanied by guitars; rhythms similar to those of South America, somewhat "Africanized" through special beats, are most popular.

LANGUAGE

The Swahili language, the most important African language in Kenya, is not as remote from English as one might expect. Some Swahili words have already been

KENYA INFORMATION SERVICES

Interesting horns such as this one are used with traditional dances and songs.

adopted in American speech—such as the words *safari* (trip or journey) and *impala* (a swift antelope). Swahili is also the *lingua franca,* or common language, of eastern and central Africa. The presence of many tribes with different tribal languages and dialects makes communication difficult unless there is a language that can be used by all. The Swahili language, rather than a foreign colonial language such as English, is the natural choice for this purpose.

Swahili is the most important language south of the Sahara. It belongs to the

All types of English books—even comic books—are available in Kenya.

LITERATURE

Bantu family of languages, a large group that includes most of the languages from Zaïre and Kenya all the way to South Africa.

All types of English books are available in the bookstores and libraries of Kenya. Those of an educational character, such as scientific and literary works, are available in the school libraries. The earlier Swahili books were generally translations from English. Many of these were educational or religious books. Since independence several noteworthy African writers have appeared on the literary scene, such as Grace Ogot, author of *Promised Land,* and James Ngugi, well known for his novels *Weep Not Child* and *A Grain of Wheat.* Some new Kenyan novels have been written in English while others have been written in Swahili.

Most of the people in Kenya can read Swahili, and the governments of the Soviet Union and the People's Republic of China have taken advantage of that fact. They have been producing a great many books ranging from well-illustrated children's readers and storybooks to political and technical material, all in Swahili. No good books in Swahili have been produced yet in the United States.

SPORTS AND ATHLETICS

The people of Kenya have always loved sports. Almost every school of junior high level and up has a good program in athletics, including running, jumping, relay racing, weight lifting, and javelin throwing. The most popular game is football, which in Kenya is the game Americans call soccer. Football matches take place all year—between schools, between special national civic groups or organizations, and between Kenya and its neighboring countries such as Uganda and Tanzania. Both the English and Swahili-language newspapers devote a page to football and athletics.

Kenya has won several silver and gold Olympic medals in athletics. One of Kenya's earliest champions was Wilson Kiprugut, who won a bronze medal in the Olympics of 1964 which were held in Tokyo, Japan. His success stimulated further interest and training, which led to astounding successes and record-breaking performances by other Kenya athletes.

In the track and field competition at the 1968 Olympic Games held in Mexico

Because Kenyans love sports, most secondary schools have good athletic programs.

Kipchoge Keino.

City, Mexico, a Kenya runner, Kipchoge Keino, set a new Olympic record in the 1,500-meter run. Keino ran this distance in 3 minutes, 34.9 seconds. Also in the 1968 Olympics, Amos Biwott won the 3,000-meter steeplechase and Naftali Temu won the 10,000-meter run.

Keino also ran in the 1,500-meter run in the 1972 Olympics in Münich, Germany —and won again.

EAST AFRICAN SAFARI

An annual sports event that is quite popular in Kenya is the East African Safari. A motor rally (and race) that attracts enthusiasts from many parts of the world, it was first run in 1953 in honor of the coronation of Great Britain's Queen Elizabeth II. Originally called the Coronation Safari, after independence the name was changed to the East African Safari. The rally is run at Eastertime and lasts three days.

The rally has many keen Indian participants. In 1965 it was won by Joginder Singh and his partner, Jaswat Singh. Lately Africans have become more enthusiastic about the sport and have started the Kenya Rallye Drivers' Club.

The East African Safari travels over a course of about three thousand miles through Kenya, Tanzania, and Uganda. It is a grueling race over miles of twisting hairpin bends, mud, and so much dust that the drivers can hardly see where they are going. The course runs from high altitudes of more than nine thousand feet down to sea level, through areas abounding in wildlife and big game (which can be real hazards), and over some stretches of paved roads where drivers can gain extra speed. Of the hundred or more cars that enter the race, only about ten or twenty usually finish. Drivers travel in pairs, taking turns at driving day and night for the whole stretch. They are allowed a brief halfway stop for rest and a few other short stops. It is a tremendous test for both car and driver, and many participants consider it a greater honor to win in the East African Safari than in some other international races.

People Work in Kenya

EAST AFRICAN COMMUNITY

Since all three major east African countries—Kenya, Tanzania, and Uganda—were under the British flag in colonial times, it has been difficult to separate Kenya's economy from that of the others. For many years these countries enjoyed common transportation and communication service, such as mail, railways and harbors, East African Airways, customs, and telecommunication, and there were no trade barriers.

Since these countries realized the advantage of close cooperation, on December 1, 1967, a treaty was signed establishing the East African Economic Community. The main signers were the three presidents: President Kenyatta of Kenya, President Nyerere of Tanzania, and President Obote of Uganda.

The headquarters of the East African Economic Community was established in Arusha, Tanzania, and its various services were divided among the three member nations. Though this arrangement has been beneficial to all the member countries, there have, of course, been some problems, especially in the important matter of "Transfer Tax." The purpose of this tax is to equalize the growth and development of the three countries, preventing one or the other from getting very rich while others fell behind in their economic

Many Kenyans work on farms near their villages.

Tourists can view Kenya's wild animals from above at Treetop Hotel near Nyeri.

growth. This difficult task of equalization is to be accomplished without discouraging individual initiative.

TOURISM

Though agriculture or mining would ordinarily be Kenya's top industry, at present tourism heads the list because of the wealth and variety of wild animals, big game, and scenic attractions. Tourists travel to Kenya from all over the world, sometimes to hunt, but most often to see, photograph, and enjoy the animals in their natural habitat.

In order to preserve the wild animals, several large game parks and national parks have been set aside. No hunting is permitted in these parks. Comfortable hotels and game lodges are situated in strategic places where visitors can enjoy and study the great variety of animals and birds, large and small, that Kenya has to offer. Kenya has more than ten national parks located in varied altitudes and climatic ranges.

One of the largest game parks is the Tsavo National Park, which covers more than eight thousand square miles. Another very popular park is the Nairobi National Park, popular mainly because it is close to the capital city of Nairobi. This park is accessible by car and one can easily drive to it from Nairobi to watch various animals for an afternoon. The lions, which have become accustomed to cars, can be observed from very close range.

In addition to the large parks, there are special game reserves, smaller parks, and historical sites. Treetop Hotel near Nyeri on the slopes of Mount Kenya is world famous. Many well-known people have visited there, spending the night up in the treetop lookout from which they can watch elephants, rhinoceroses, buffalos, antelopes, warthogs, and other animals drinking at the pool below the tree.

The Kenyan government has taken advantage of its animal resource and is making life for tourists as attractive as possible. Kenya's lakes, streams, and rivers all provide excellent fishing. Attractive holiday resorts have been built at the tropical ocean beaches and more people are discovering the natural beauties of the country. The tourists also bring much money which they spend in Kenya, thus contributing to its economy. It is said that holidays in Kenya do not end and that every month is a special holiday month.

CROPS

Much of the fertile highland region is ideally suited for growing coffee and tea. These have become Kenya's most important cash crops. Coffee is the second largest industry, next to tourism. Crops have brought as much as £15 million (42 million United States dollars) in the best

Men picking red berries in a coffee plantation. These berries contain the beans used to make coffee.

KENYA INFORMATION SERVICES

years. Kenya is not too worried about competition from Brazil, the largest coffee grower in the world, because Kenya grows a special kind of coffee not grown in Brazil.

It is a delight to walk through a coffee plantation, especially when the short, bushy trees are covered with millions of clusters of snow-white, fragrant flowers. Later in the season, the blossoms give way to small, cherrylike fruit, which turns red when ripe. The berries must be hand-picked. They contain coffee beans, which are processed to be cured and dried before the coffee is sent to the markets of the world.

Tea growing and processing is quite an art—much more involved than coffee growing. At just the right time, just the right leaves must be picked and then cured. With a good rainfall, the tea estates in the high altitudes flourish. Kericho in western Kenya is the most important tea growing region; it is known all over the world for its tea. The tea crop brings to Kenya about £10 million (US $28 million) a year.

Another very important crop, grown on a smaller scale, is maize (Indian corn), a staple, or basic, food in much of Africa. Maize is grown almost totally for domestic consumption. In the highlands the dainty, daisylike flower called pyrethrum has been grown in considerable quantities; from this flower comes pyrethrin, used in insect sprays. In the lowlands many farmers grow sisal, a hemplike fiber used in many industries. Unfortunately, sisal does not always command a good price in the marketplace. For the local markets, various vegetables and fruits, including mangoes and papayas, are grown quite successfully.

LIVESTOCK

The native cattle are a rather small breed, used mainly for meat rather than for dairy products. The modern cattle rancher in Kenya is constantly fighting ticks and tsetse flies—common problems in tropical areas. The tsetse fly, a type of horsefly, is a carrier of fatal diseases that affect cattle. Unlike many African countries, however, Kenya has now virtually eliminated the tsetse fly. Periodically the ticks are killed off by "dipping" the cattle in a concrete trough filled with water deep enough so that the cow must swim through it. Certain chemicals added to the water kill whatever ticks may be on the cow's hide. Many ranchers have also imported good breeds of cattle from abroad; by crossbreeding the ranchers have upgraded Kenya's cattle. The fine breeds of cattle now available in Kenya are shown at an annual agricultural show held near Nairobi. The best cattle are raised in the highlands; that is also where the few fine dairy herds are kept.

There is an increasing number of very productive poultry farms in Kenya and new breeds of poultry have been imported. Now high-quality eggs are available for the markets as well as fryer chickens for the large demand in homes and hotels.

This tribesman stands near his sheep. Behind him are some huts in his compound.

Wool-bearing sheep have been imported from other countries, especially Australia and New Zealand; a very successful beginning has been made in this industry. Most of the wool is being bought by a blanket factory at Nakuru and very fine woolen blankets are being produced there.

For many years pigs have been raised quite successfully. At the Uplands bacon factory, about twenty-five miles north of Nairobi, much of the pork, bacon, sausage, and lard is processed and prepared for marketing.

TRANSPORTATION

Outside of Nairobi is a very fine international airport which accommodates airplanes of all sizes from all nations of the world. Traffic is brisk and passengers to Nairobi have an interesting ride from the airport into the city; the road follows a route near Nairobi National Park.

Kenya's railways are part of the East African Railway system, combining with branches and mainlines in Tanzania and Uganda. No expansion of the railroad has

Above: Many dirt highways are now being paved. Below: Bridges span ocean inlets where ferries once brought cars and passengers across.

Nairobi's busy airport accommodates planes from all over the world.

taken place recently in Kenya, as more emphasis has been placed on building new highways. A branch line of the railroad goes north to Lake Magadi, carting away the profitable salt and soda ash mined in that region.

Many dirt highways are now being improved or paved. Good main highways have long led into Tanzania and Uganda because Kenya's highway system was closely integrated with these two countries. Lately, however, Kenya has begun to expand its road system in other directions as well. A major new development is the building of a paved highway from Kenya north to Addis Ababa in Ethiopia, the first road connection between these two na-

tions. Air traffic between Kenya and Ethiopia developed only in the 1960s. In addition to the above, a transcontinental highway is planned from Kenya through Uganda and Zaïre all the way into Nigeria on the west coast. Such an undertaking will require the joint cooperation of all the nations involved.

SHIPPING

With its fine coastline, Kenya can boast of having one of the best and largest ports in east Africa, the port of Mombasa. Mombasa township and harbor facilities are located on an island neatly set in a

77

large bay. The south channel is deep enough to permit large oceangoing vessels to enter and the deep-water harbor, Kilindini Harbor, is well protected on the inland side of the island. Thirteen large ships plus a number of oil tankers can anchor in Kilindini Harbor at the same time. Traffic in the port of Mombasa is heavy; in 1970 about two thousand ships called at this port. Kenya is also in partnership with other eastern African countries in operating a shipping line.

Kenya operates a few large lake steamers on Lake Victoria. Kenya's main port on Lake Victoria is Kisumu; this port is equipped with workshops and drydocks to service the steamers. Passengers can take a leisurely and comfortable five-day steamer cruise around the lake. The steamer calls at several lake ports in Uganda and Tanzania before returning to Kisumu.

COMMUNICATIONS

In the United States private firms handle all telegrams, but in Kenya there is no separate agency for that purpose. All telegrams are sent by the post office. The large aerials and towers on top of the main post office building in Nairobi are an indication of this service. In addition to handling mail and telegrams, the post office also provides facilities for post office savings accounts. At the post office one can buy stamps that represent either Kenya alone or all three nations of the East African Community.

Radio broadcasting services in Kenya are not privately owned as they are in the United States; instead, radio broadcasting is operated by the Kenya government through the Ministry of Information and Broadcasting. The Voice of Kenya radio has full daily programming in both English and Swahili, plus some shows in local languages.

The first television station was built in October, 1962. The output of television shows reached about forty hours per week in 1970; shows were broadcast in both English and Swahili. A second television station was built in Mombasa in 1969.

INDUSTRY

Industries have been somewhat slow in establishing themselves in Kenya. It is only during the last two or three decades that they have slowly been built up. Electric power became increasingly available and more foreign aid and investments came to Kenya after independence. Because of this, quite a few new industries were developed and some of the older ones were expanded, including a blanket factory; a division of Union Carbide, an American corporation; a plastics manufacturer; a cement factory near Mombasa; and a large shoe factory in Limuru. Large manufacturers of tires and rubber products, textiles, radios, tools and appliances, pulp and paper, and pottery, along with many other smaller manufacturers, are producing enough to make Kenya fairly

Young people work together, spinning thread and weaving beautiful blankets of varied colors and patterns.

independent as far as internal needs are concerned. Kenya also produces good quality beer and soft drinks. Heavier products, however, such as automobiles, trucks, tractors, and heavy machinery, must be imported from abroad.

Smaller industries that depend on the handcraft and skills of African craftsmen have existed in Kenya for a long time. The Kamba people (who live east of Nairobi) and many of the Kikuyu have become

adept at carving and fashioning wood sculpture, especially figurines of animals. Both graceful and attractive, these are in great demand by visitors and tourists. These carvings have become well known abroad and are now available in souvenir shops in many parts of the world. Considering the patience and skill required to fashion and carve out each piece, it is amazing that literally thousands have become available for export.

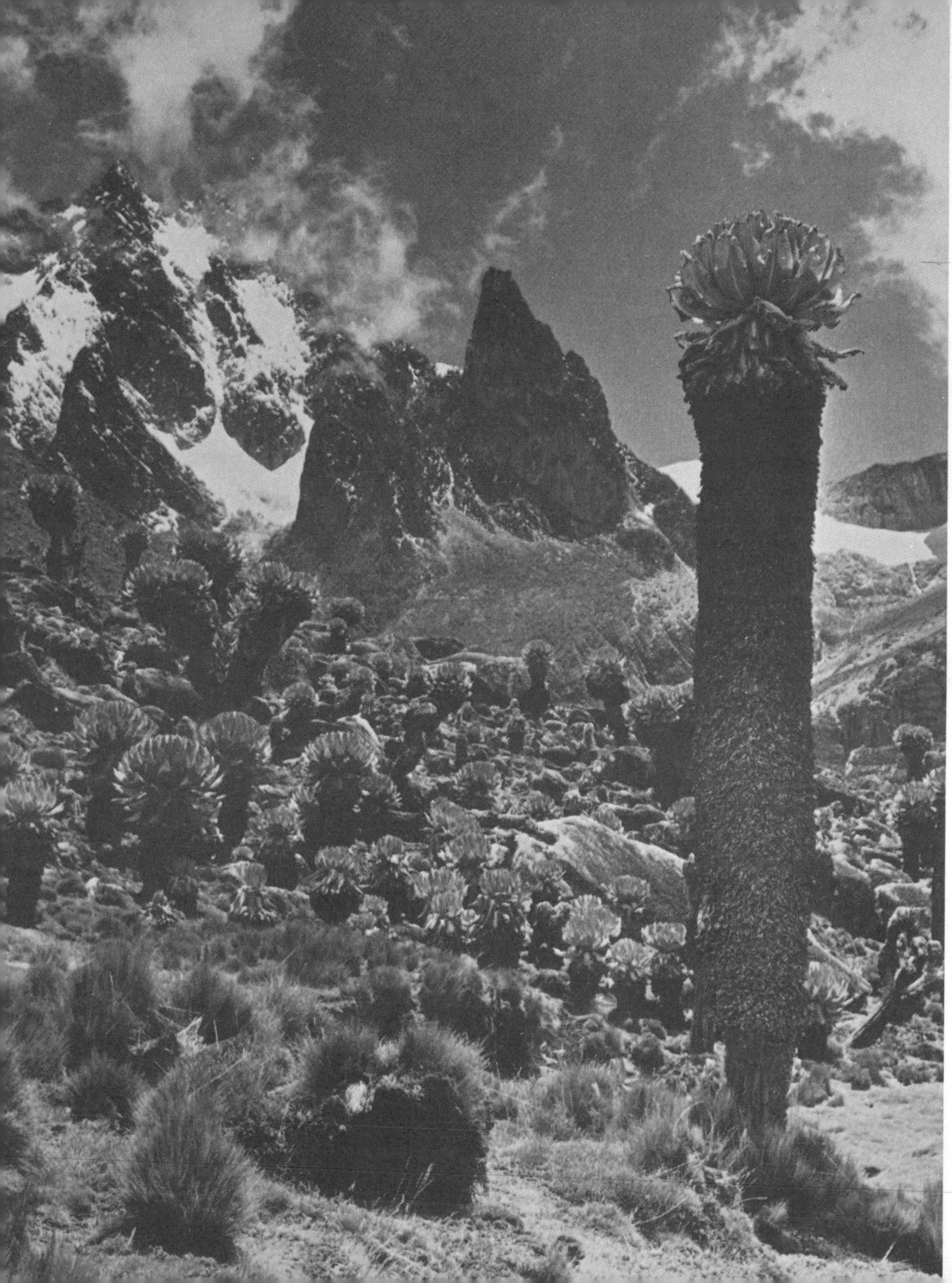

EAST AFRICAN RAILWAYS AND HARBORS

Enchantment of Kenya

A GREAT ACCOMPLISHMENT

This true story of three Italian prisoners of war illustrates very clearly the enchantment of the land of Kenya.

During World War II, the three Italians were kept in a prison camp outside of Nanyuki; every day they feasted their eyes on the beauty of Mount Kenya towering above them. Day after day the enchantment of this majestic mountain became stronger, until they could resist it no longer. The three friends secretly started to hoard some of their food rations and when they felt they had enough, managed to leave camp without being observed. Their goal was to climb to the very top of this magnificent mountain.

During their journey up the mountain they passed through the dense forest of the lower slopes, encountered wild animals, slept without shelter in the open, climbed through Alpine meadows with exquisite flowers, then passed through an area with little vegetation—only rocks, snow, and glaciers. They climbed these treacherous slopes—without a guide—until they actually reached the top and planted the Italian flag there. It was truly an amazing accomplishment.

The three Italians then climbed down the mountain and found their way back to the prison camp—hungry and exhausted, yet filled with the satisfaction of having accomplished such a feat. The lure and fascination of that great mountain which the

Giant groundsel on the slopes of Mount Kenya. Though the three prisoners were not the first to climb Mount Kenya, their journey was a daring one.

Africans regarded as the abode of the gods now had become part of the three men. They had spent nearly eighteen days on this journey. Back in camp they dutifully reported to the commandant and told him what they had done. Though no one believed them, they had a diary, and for all who cared to climb up and see, the Italian flag was flying on top of the mountain as proof of their journey.

Kenya's charm and exquisite beauty has lured thousands of foreign visitors to its hills and flatlands. Some have enjoyed it so much that they stayed, making their homes in this distant land. Most people arrive in Kenya for the first time at the Nairobi airport. The ride from the airport into the city has its own attractions, as passengers are sometimes greeted by giraffes, zebras, and antelopes standing near the roads. On the outskirts of the city the road, called Uhuru Highway (formerly Princess Elizabeth Way), is flanked by flowers, flowering bushes, bougainvillea, and palms. Nairobi can also be approached by way of the paved motor highway from the port of Mombasa. From Nairobi this road follows the railway line, winding through the Rift Valley and down to Lake Victoria.

The heart of Nairobi is cut by Kenyatta Avenue, a street with stately buildings; on the median strip is a flowering row of jacaranda trees. As in any major city, there are areas in Nairobi that are not so beautiful; generally, however, the many modern buildings, some over ten stories high, make one forget that this is actually the heart of Africa, only a few miles south of the equator. Nairobi's "garden city" image is continued in the uncrowded residential suburbs, where each attractive home is surrounded by clumps of trees and shrubs and masses of flowers.

THE SCENIC HIGHLANDS

At an altitude of 5,452 feet above sea level, Nairobi is the gateway to the famous highlands of Kenya. A rail branch line and

Gazelle graze along the roadside near Nairobi. Sometimes they can be seen crossing the road.

MICHAEL ROBERTS

Nairobi is the gateway to the scenic highlands.

a paved highway extend northeast from the city into the foothills of Mount Kenya, where they reach Nyeri (6,200 feet above sea level). The generous rainfall provides for an abundance of flowering plants and trees, along with an evergreen golf course that invites the keen golfer year round. A side trip to Treetops Hotel is an experience in itself, since big game and interesting animals can be found almost anywhere nearby.

Leaving Nyeri, majestic Mount Kenya beckons; what better place to find a location fit as a gift for a queen? Tucked away in the primeval forest is Kenya's gift to the queen of England—Sagana Lodge, with expertly landscaped grounds. When Queen Elizabeth of England first visited there she was still Princess Elizabeth; during her stay her pleasure quickly turned to sorrow at news of her father's death. She immediately left for England to be crowned queen. After Kenya's independence, Queen Elizabeth accepted the government's invitation to return to the beautiful lodge in the woods.

About thirty miles from Nyeri is the small community of Nanyuki; the road between the two towns crosses the equator. The Silverbeck Hotel is right on the equator. It is said that visitors having a drink at the bar there can stand with one foot in the Northern Hemisphere and the other in the Southern Hemisphere.

A few miles past Nanyuki toward Mount Kenya is American film star William Holden's luxurious and spacious lodge, presently known as the Mount Kenya Safari Club. The spacious gardens, the golden-crested cranes and flamingos in the ornamental pool, huge, multicolored flowering poinsettias, and snow-covered Mount Kenya in the distance all add to the beauty of the place.

Northward from Nairobi is the town of Limuru, where at times frost can be seen on the ground early in the mornings and where plums and pears can be bought in the market when in season. Often when the passenger train stops at Limuru, the local people come to the station to sell their fruit to the passengers. From Limuru the railroad winds down to the edge of the Rift Valley, where two mountains rise from the floor of the valley. These are Mount Suswa and Mount Longonot, both with extinct volcanic craters.

The heights reached on the western side of the valley at Timboroa (nine thousand feet above sea level) are bracing and exhilarating. The early morning frost makes it hard to believe that the peak is on the equator. The road continues to Eldoret where Mount Elgon, Kenya's second highest mountain, is visible in the distance.

Mount Elgon is on the boundary between Kenya and Uganda; it is an extinct volcano 14,178 feet high. At certain times of the year snow can be seen on the top, but it soon melts away. To have a closer look at this interesting mountain, one must go farther north to the small township and farming community of Kitale. From there one can drive into the forest belt of Mount Elgon, where elephants and buffalo abound and often wander right onto the roadway.

A LOOK SOUTHWARD

The main North-South Road extends to the Tanzania border. On this road is the town of Namanga, with a picturesque small hotel; here the atmosphere is relaxing and refreshments are good. At Namanga is the turn-off to one of Kenya's most fascinating game parks, Amboseli National Park on the Tanzania border. Along this road can be seen men of the Masai tribe, their skins painted with red ocher. They usually stand on one leg with the other propped against the knee of the first and lean against a long spear. Masai men braid their hair tightly and cover it heavily with reddish clay and grease. For clothing they wear a piece of leather or cloth loosely hitched over one shoulder. They very seldom speak and their bearing is dignified. Since Amboseli National Park is located in Masailand, they have an interest in it and its preservation.

Off the road a bit a Masai *kraal,* or village, can be seen. This is a collection of dome-shaped huts plastered with mud and cow dung. There are no windows—just a

Small family groups of Masai travel with the seasons, building clusters of elongated huts.

low door. These huts, known as *manyata,* are surrounded by a high enclosure of thorn branches that keep predatory animals outside and the kraal's cattle inside. One of the staple foods of the Masai is cow's blood mixed with milk and left to turn sour; it is kept in a long gourd. The necessary amount of blood is drawn from a vein in the cow's neck, which is sealed up again; this apparently does not harm the cow.

The most abundant animals in the park are rhinoceroses and elephants. One of the special attractions of Amboseli National Park is the presence of Africa's highest mountain, Mount Kilimanjaro, across the Tanzanian border. Towering into the skies to an altitude of 19,400 feet and covered with eternal ice and snow, this majestic mountain dominates the scene for many miles around.

There is a legend told that many, many years ago King Menelik of Ethiopia (of the lineage of King Solomon and the Queen of Sheba) took a long journey south to meet another king. On his way back

King Menelik became seriously ill and knew he would die. He and his caravan camped at the foot of Mount Kilimanjaro; looking up at the grandeur above, Menelik felt that this mountain would be the only fitting burial place for him. He then commanded his men to take him as far to the top as possible and bury him there when he died. They followed his command, burying him somewhere in the high reaches of the mountain, together with much of his royal treasure.

On his finger the king was said to have worn a special ring inherited from King Solomon. This ring, set with a sparkling precious blue stone, was reputed to have the power to grant to whomever wore it the gift of much wisdom and the answer to many riddles and problems. If the ring really existed, it is now lost forever, buried under the drifting snows.

When the moon is full, the glittering snows of Mount Kilimanjaro above and the nearby silhouettes of the flat-topped acacias are visible from the porch of the Amboseli Lodge. Piercing the night is the occasional growl or roar of a lion or the sight of a browsing elephant or rhinoceros seeking a water hole.

THE COASTAL LANDS

The historic coast of Kenya is washed by waves from the Indian Ocean. Mombasa, the main port, is famous for its relics of past dominions. Fort Jesus, built by the Portuguese in 1593, still stands on Mombasa Island, a reminder of the days when the Portuguese were influential in this part of the world. The narrow, winding streets of the Arab quarter and the ornate Arab High School tell of when these people dominated. The modern buildings in Mombasa, including the Hotel Oceanic that overlooks the ocean and harbor, tell of the strong influence that Western civilization has had on Africa.

Salim Road, in the business section of Mombasa, has scarlet trees growing in its median strip. Under the trees, Kamba craftsmen display their fine wood carvings of various animals and people. In between sales they are busy carving, using very simple tools, yet producing beautiful figurines. Running into Salim Road is Station Road, on which there are some modern businesses, hotels, and restaurants. Station Road leads down to Kilindini harbor, where ships from nations all over the world are anchored.

South of Mombasa the coastline is especially attractive, with many coconut palms, resorts, and sunny beaches. At Kwale, away from the thorny bushland which lies behind the coastal belt, is a region of hills. These are the Shimba Hills, an area of which has been designated as a national reserve. This region is famous for a specialty not found anywhere else in Kenya—the rare and magnificent sable antelope. This beautiful beast stands five feet high and is almost pure black, with great curved horns.

North of Mombasa more historic monuments can be seen, as well as small, attractive seaside towns and resorts. A

Sisal to be exported is being loaded on one of the many ships that visit Mombasa's Kilindini Harbor each month.

beautiful paved highway makes traveling from Mombasa to Malindi a short and simple trip. Bridges now span ocean inlets where ferries once brought cars and passengers across. The ferrymen, pulling the ferry across by rope, sang merrily, often making up songs about their passengers as the boat crossed over to the other side.

The first large township north of Mombasa is Kilifi. Here is a larger ocean inlet that is deep enough for small ships and sailing vessels. According to legend, in olden days smugglers and pirates used Kilifi as their secret landing place and even smuggled ivory out of there. To this day there are many elephants in the wooded areas just north of the town, but Kilifi is now a pleasant small town and administrative center for the region. In the surrounding area pineapples are grown in large quantities; there is a pineapple canning factory in Kilifi. Cashew nuts and coconuts are also grown in quantities and some experimentation is being made with

GEDI, THE PALACE

The mysterious, but lovely, palace at Gedi.

macadamia nuts imported from Hawaii. Perhaps these, too, may prove to be a valuable crop for Kenya in the future.

A few more miles up the coast the charming old town of Malindi welcomes the visitor. A pleasant place with a large, curving beach and clean sand, it has been nicknamed the "Riviera of Kenya." Quite a number of excellent hotels provide accommodation for tourists. Here Vasco da Gama's pillar-shaped monument tells of his visit in 1648. It is also here that a satellite launching station has been erected with the help of the United States.

THE MYSTERY CITY

About ten miles south of Malindi, between the main road and the ocean, lie the ruins of the "Lost City of Gedi"—lost for centuries in the forest, lost in all known records, and lost to the memory of man. No one even knows who built it, when, or why it was so mysteriously abandoned. Yet its architecture speaks of an advanced civilization and the beauty of workmanship in the masonry is remarkable.

From earliest times none of the explorers of the east coast of Africa—Arabs, Portuguese, English, or Persian—mention Gedi anywhere in their records, though Malindi, Kilifi, and Mombasa are almost always mentioned. The visitor to the coastal region of Kenya soon shares the feeling of mystery that surrounds Gedi. Was Gedi its original name? What catastrophe made the inhabitants leave without trace or record?

Presently Gedi is a National Historical Monument; archaeologists have explored it from time to time without discovering much. The most recent theory is that Gedi is more than eight hundred years old and was probably built by Persians. Some of the pottery found there, however, is of a Chinese type. The "legendary" Sinbad the Sailor (who really existed) reported to Sultan Haroun al Rashid about places along the east coast of Africa. Did he know about Gedi? Many experts feel that he did.

The ruins now being dug out of the forest that has taken possession of the lost city indicate that at one time this must have been a thriving place—with a palace, a mosque or temple, and other important monuments and structures. It is presumed that in the area between Kilifi and Malindi there may be even more such ruins buried in the forests where elephants now roam. All this mystery of Kenya's coastline add to the natural enchantment of Kenya.

In the area between Kilifi and Malindi the ocean waters are exceptionally clear and rich in marine life, such as in the Blue Lagoon just south of Gedi, and several other places which have been designated Marine National Parks. No fishing is allowed, but swimmers with underwater goggles and scuba gear may have a rewarding experience exploring these ocean gardens.

The variety of climate, the grandeur and scenic beauty of such regions as the highlands, Mount Kenya, and the ocean beaches, the variety and richness of life, and the many contrasts and mysteries partially explain the fascination and enchantment of a land which has tremendous potential for the future.

FACING THE FUTURE

The new Kenya has risen nobly to its many problems and challenges and confidently faces the future. In the spirit of "harambee!" much is accomplished. Kenya's national anthem reveals the idealism and spirit of the enchanted land which is Kenya.

WIMBO WA TAIFA

Ee Mu – ngu ngu – vu ye – tu I – le – te ba – ra – ka
kwe – tu Ha – ki i – we nga – o na mli – nzi na – tu ka – e na u – du – gu A–
–ma – ni na u – hu – ru Ra – ha tu – pa – te na u – sta – wi

Amkeni ndugu zetu
Tufanye sote bidii
Nasi tujitoe kwa nguvu
Nchi yetu ya Kenya,
Tunayoipenda
Tuwe tayari kulinda.

Natujenge taifa letu
Ee, ndio wajibu wetu
Kenya istahili heshima
Tuungane mikono
Pomoja kazini
Kila siku puwe na shukrani.

NATIONAL ANTHEM

O God of all cre — a—tion Bless this our land and
na—tion Jus—tice be our shield and de — fen — der May we dwell in u—ni — ty
Peace and lib—er — ty Plen — ty be found with—in our bor—ders

Let one and all arise
With hearts both strong and true.
Service be our earnest endeavor,
and our Homeland of Kenya,
Heritage of splendor,
Firm may we stand to defend.

Let all with one accord
In common bond united,
Build this our nation together
and the glory of Kenya
The fruit of our labor
Fill every heart with thanksgiving.

Handy Reference Section

INSTANT FACTS

Political:

Official Name—Republic of Kenya
Capital—Nairobi
Official Languages—Swahili and English
Literacy Rate—30 percent
Monetary Units: 1 Kenya Shilling (Sh.) = 100 cents
      20 Kenya Sh. = 1 Kenya Pound (K£)
      1 Kenya Pound = US $2.80
Flag—Three horizontal stripes (black, red, and green) from top to bottom, separated by very narrow white stripes or bands. A warrior's shield and crossed spears are centered on the flag.

Geographical:

Area—224,960 square miles
Greatest Length—about 600 miles (north to south)
Greatest Width—about 535 miles (east to west)
Highest Point—Mount Kenya (17,058 feet)
Lowest Point—sea level

PROVINCES

Province	Population	Main City
Central	1,745,000	Nyeri
Coast	950,000	Mombasa
Eastern	2,200,000	Embu
Nairobi area	510,000	Nairobi
North-Eastern	568,000	Wajir
Nyanza	1,950,000	Kisumu
Rift Valley	2,160,000	Nakuru
Western	1,415,000	Kakamega

POPULATION

Total Population—11,500,000 (1970)
Average Population Density—48.6 per square mile
Growth Rate—3.5 percent
Birth Rate—50 per 1,000
Death Rate—20 per 1,000

Principal Cities:

Eldoret	17,000
Kericho	10,900
Kisumu	30,700
Kitale	11,500
Mombasa	180,000
Nairobi	510,000
Nakuru	47,800
Nanyuki	11,000
Nyeri	10,000
Thika	18,100

HOLIDAYS AND SPECIAL EVENTS

January 1—New Year's Day
March-April—Easter, including Good Friday and Easter Monday (movable holidays)
March-April—East African Safari
May 1—Labor Day
June 1 or 2—Madaraka (Responsibility) Day (If June 1 falls on a Sunday, then Madaraka Day is June 2)
August—Bank Holiday, first Monday
August—Agricultural Show
October 20—Kenyatta Day
October-November—Id-ul-Fitr (movable holiday, for Muslims)
December 12—Jamhuri (Independence) Day
December 25—Christmas
December 26—Boxing Day

SWAHILI WORDS AND PHRASES

ni	I	*kwenda*	go
u	you (singular)	*simba*	lion
a	he, she	*hapa*	here
tu	we	*kitabu*	book
m	you (plural)	*ninapenda*	I like
wa	they	*nitapenda*	I shall like
penda	like, love	*nilipenda*	I liked
ona	see	*anaona simba*	he sees a lion
fanya	do, make	*tunaketihapa*	we are sitting here
keti	sit	*walikwenda*	they went
soma	read	*nitasoma kitabu*	I shall read a book

YOU HAVE A DATE WITH HISTORY

1000 B.C.—Bushmen and hunters inhabit Kenya

A.D. 975-1497—Period of the Zenj Empire (Arab)

1498—Vasco da Gama visits Kenya

1500-1509—Portuguese conquest of the east coast

1593—Portuguese build Fort Jesus in Mombasa

1741—Portuguese domination ends

1828—Seyyid Said introduces cloves to Zanzibar

1832—Seyyid Said becomes ruler of east Africa; Zanzibar declared the capital

1837—American consulate established

1848—J. Rebmann discovers Mount Kilamanjaro and Dr. J. B. Krapf discovers Mount Kenya

1856—Death of Seyyid Said

1869—Suez Canal opens

1872—British India Steam Navigation Company starts Aden-Zanzibar route

1873—Slave market in Zanzibar closed

1879—Undersea cable laid to Zanzibar

1888—Imperial British East Africa Company formed

1895—Kenya becomes a British Protectorate; construction starts on the Kenya-Uganda Railway

1899—Railway reaches Nairobi

1901—Railway reaches Kisumu on Lake Victoria

1920—Most of Kenya proclaimed a British Crown Colony; first elections to Legislative Council

1922—Colonial Office proposes Common Roll

1923—Settlers refuse the Common Roll; Britain states that Kenya be held in trust for the Africans

1927—Union of the three east African territories proposed, not passed

1941—Lord Baden-Powell, founder of the Boy Scouts, dies and is buried in Kenya

1944—Mr. Eliud W. Mathu becomes the first African nominated to the Legislative Council

1945—Nairobi National Game Park established

1946—Kenya African Union (KAU) is formed

1948—East African High Commission created

1952-1956—Mau Mau organization

1952—Jomo Kenyatta arrested

1953—KAU is banned; Coronation Safari first run

1957—Lennox-Boyd Constitution; first Africans elected to Legislative Council

1959—Dr. L. S. B. Leakey discovers Zinjanthropus man; African political parties permitted

1960—Kenya African National Union (KANU) and Kenya African Democratic Union (KADU) parties formed

1961—Jomo Kenyatta released from prison

1962—Television comes to Kenya

1963—General elections; internal self-government granted, June 1; Jomo Kenyatta elected as first prime minister; Kenya becomes independent, December 12

1964—Coastal strip becomes part of independent Kenya; Wilson Kiprugut wins Kenya's first Olympics medal, Tokyo; Kenya becomes a republic

1967—East African Community organized

1968—Kipchoge Keino sets record for 1,500-meter run, Amos Biwott wins 3,000-meter steeplechase, and Naftali Temu wins 10,000-meter run at Olympics, Mexico City

1969—Assassination of Tom Mboya

1971—Satellite launched from Malindi; Richard Leakey makes archaeological discoveries

1972—Keino wins 1,500-meter run at Olympics, Münich

Index

About the Author: Already the author of seventy-three books published by Childrens Press, Allan Carpenter is on his way again with the forty-two book "Enchantment of Africa" series. Except for a few years spent founding, editing, and publishing a teachers' magazine, Allan has worked as a free-lance writer of books and magazine articles. During his many years in publishing, he has perfected a highly organized approach to handling large volumes of material—after extensive traveling and having collected all possible materials, he systematically reviews and organizes everything. From his apartment high in the magnificant John Hancock Building, Allan recalls: "My collection and assimilation of materials on the states and countries began before the publication of my first book when I was twenty years old." When not writing or traveling, Allan also enjoys music—he has been the principal string bass player for the Chicago Business Men's Orchestra for twenty-five years.

Date Due

FEB 25			
MAR 4			
MAR 8			
MAR 21			
March W			
APR 9			
NOV 21			
MAR 28			
MAR 4			
NOV 23			
3/80			
3/30			
FEB 24 78			
MAR 6 78			